"If you know a teenager, you'll want to get this book in their hands. It will help them navigate the tricky waters they face today and build an identity that will last a lifetime. And I think parents who read it will learn a thing or two as well."

—Dennis Rainey, Founder and CEO, FamilyLife

"This book is bursting with wisdom. I've rarely come across a text that will more reshape life and thought for people pulled by a fallen world than this one. It's fun to read, it's chock-full of engaging stories, and it will connect with young readers. This is a book the entire student-group should read—and discuss, and pray over, and figure out how to practice in everyday life. We believe in a big God, a big Christ, and the satisfaction of a transformed life, and this book shows the way."

—Dr. Owen Strachan, author, *Risky Gospel*;
Associate Professor of Christian Theology,
Midwestern Baptist Theological Seminary

"The background elevator music to all of our lives centers around the question of identity. Everyone will search for identity. Sadly most will end up in the wrong place. *True Identity* offers hope and points us to the only true source of identity. Because the issue John deals with is a universal one, this book is for everyone."

—Bryan Loritts, lead pastor, Abundant Life Christian
Fellowship; author, *Saving the Saved*

"*True Identity* is an inviting call to embrace, nurture, and celebrate who God intended for us to be. Thanks, John, for the compelling way in which you point us back to the ultimate source of identity, Jesus Christ."

—Dr. Crawford W. Loritts Jr, author, speaker, radio host, and
senior pastor, Fellowship Bible Church, Roswell, Georgia

"I wish this book had been available for me to read when I was in high school! It's packed with a lot of deep wisdom about life and illustrated with fascinating personal stories. And it's all solidly grounded in the teachings of the Bible. I highly recommend it!"

—Wayne Grudem, PhD, Research Professor of Theology and Biblical Studies, Phoenix Seminary, Scottsdale, Arizona

"As a father of three teenagers, I believe it is critical that we engage our children on their true identity in Christ. I pray for us as Christian parents that we won't try to hide from the battles facing our teens, but instead be courageous and fight for their hearts."

—Jason Houser, founder, Seeds Family Worship Ministry; author, *Dedicated: Training Children to Trust and Follow Jesus*

"The transition from childhood to adulthood is tough for teens. And the messages young people are hearing in our culture are making that transition significantly more challenging. My friend and colleague John Majors cuts through the haze with skillful, biblical clarity to help teens answer the question, 'Exactly who am I, anyway?'"

—Bob Lepine, co-host, FamilyLife Today

TRUE
IDENTITY

TRUE IDENTITY

FINDING SIGNIFICANCE AND FREEDOM THROUGH WHO YOU ARE IN CHRIST

JOHN C. MAJORS

BETHANYHOUSE

a division of Baker Publishing Group
Minneapolis, Minnesota

Published by Bethany House Publishers
11400 Hampshire Avenue South
Bloomington, Minnesota 55438
www.bethanyhouse.com

Bethany House Publishers is a division of
Baker Publishing Group, Grand Rapids, Michigan

Printed in the United States of America

Library of Congress Control Number: 2017945990

ISBN 978-0-7642-3014-1

Unless otherwise indicated, Scripture quotations are from the New American Standard Bible®, copyright © 1960, 1962, 1963, 1968, 1971, 1972, 1973, 1975, 1977, 1995 by The Lockman Foundation. Used by permission. (www.Lockman.org)

Scripture quotations identified ESV are from The Holy Bible, English Standard Version® (ESV®), copyright © 2001 by Crossway, a publishing ministry of Good News Publishers. Used by permission. All rights reserved. ESV Text Edition: 2011

Scripture quotations identified HCSB are from the Holman Christian Standard Bible®, copyright © 1999, 2000, 2002, 2003, 2009 by Holman Bible Publishers. Used by permission. Holman Christian Standard Bible®, Holman CSB®, and HCSB® are federally registered trademarks of Holman Bible Publishers.

Scripture quotations identified NIV are from the Holy Bible, New International Version®. NIV®. Copyright © 1973, 1978, 1984, 2011 by Biblica, Inc.™ Used by permission of Zondervan. All rights reserved worldwide. www.zondervan.com

Some names and identifying details have been changed to protect the privacy of those involved.

Cover design by LOOK Design Studio

Author is represented by Wolgemuth & Associates

17 18 19 20 21 22 23   7 6 5 4 3 2 1

In memory of Daryl Brown,
a true friend

Contents

WHO AM I?

Alecia Faith Pennington, a young woman about your age, had dreams: She wanted to travel and see the world. First, she needed to get a job and start saving for this dream. But there was a problem: She didn't exist. At least, not in the government's eyes. She had been born at home and her parents hadn't filed the usual paperwork, so she had no birth certificate. And since she didn't have a birth certificate, she had no social security number. She'd never really been to the doctor or dentist, so she had no medical or dental records. And she was homeschooled, so she had no public records there. She also had no driver's license. Basically anything the government would use to establish her citizenship, she didn't have. In their eyes, she had no identity. And this wasn't a hundred years ago; this was within the last few years.[1]

How do you convince the government that you really exist when you have no proof? Trying to figure this out involved lawyers, judges, and even her state's legislature. But it also created a host of questions for Alecia—like, *Who am I, really? What is my* true *identity? Who am I at my very core?*

Even though Alecia didn't have the right paperwork, she really did exist and had an identity of some kind.

We all have things that have shaped who we are. They've given us an identity up to this point. But how do we discover our true identity—the truest sense of self? That's the difference between who we already are and who we really want to be.

So how do you discover your true identity? That's an enormous question, and it's what this book is going to tackle.

1

What Is Identity?

ry to think back to when you were two years old. Remember anything? That gross feeling of walking around in a saggy diaper? Having low self-esteem due to your enormous toddler belly and short arms? A lack of balance and self-confidence because of your colossal noggin? How does anyone survive that time emotionally?

You survived because you don't remember any of it. Not only that, but at that age, you don't care what other people think of you. You never stop and wonder if you'll make a difference in this world or if anyone will remember you after you die . . . life is simple and carefree. In fact, my three-year-old is never happier than when he's running through the house naked and unashamed. Once he gains freedom from the shackles of clothing, he'll fight like a cornered timber wolf to keep them off.

But somewhere around age five, things start to change. Children notice when people make fun of them or whether or not they are succeeding. They start to think, *Is that my fault? Should I act differently? Will people like me more if I* [fill in the blank]? Something has changed: self-awareness is developing.

This sense of self keeps growing through the middle teen years, when you start to ask yourself big questions like, *What am I good at? Do people like me? Will I make a difference in this world?* and *Will anyone even remember me?*

And the real biggies: *What makes me,* me? *What shapes the core of who I am?*

Wrestling with these questions can be exciting, but it can also hit you like a sucker punch—coming out of nowhere—leaving you dazed and confused, wondering what you did to deserve it, and asking, *Why can't I just go back to my three-year-old naked and blissful self?*

Why It's Important to Understand Your Identity

No, you don't want to go back there. Would you really want to go through potty training again? The questions you have are real and have to be dealt with. But here's the cool part—wrestling with these questions *now* can make a big difference. Developing an understanding *now* of who you are, of what you want out of life, of what you really value at your core, will help you shape your life for the future.

Understanding your identity is also important because *who you are determines what you do.* You will act like who you are. And the more you intentionally shape your identity, the more your actions will reflect the person you want to be. Having a clear sense of identity is having integrity; meaning, you act, live, and think in a way that matches the way you view yourself.

But if you don't have that, it creates confusion, chaos, and inner turmoil. And it can feed an identity crisis.

I had a friend in high school who was well-liked by everyone and was a pretty serious athlete. But he had a huge car wreck that he barely survived, and his athleticism disappeared. His sense of identity crumbled and he struggled with depression and anger toward God. If your identity is based on something that can be taken away, it can crumble in a hurry. But if it is based on something more enduring, you'll have a better chance of weathering an identity crisis.

So how do you get that? How do you get a clear sense of identity? And how do you get an identity based in something that will endure?

Well, before answering that, we first need to start by understanding how your identity gets shaped, because there's so much more to it than we often realize.

What Shapes Your Identity?

Identity is a complex thing. If someone asks "Who are you?" what do you tell them? Your name? That's a good start. But that's not all. Your identity includes things like your age; your likes and dislikes; your hobbies and sports; your favorite books, games, movies, food; and maybe the influence of famous people like sports stars or actors. Drop in a favorite Bible verse or two and, of course, don't forget the detailed list of your most revered figures of the sixteenth-century Magisterial Reformation. (Okay . . . maybe not that . . .)

The point is, there's a whole host of things that go into shaping who you are. Like a deck of cards, they all play a part of the game. But like a deck of cards, some have more significance than others.

Family

Americans tend to think they are self-made. They went out and tracked down their identity, grabbed it by the hair, dragged it back to the cave, and owned it. But some of your most defining characteristics—the things most central to your identity—you really had nothing to do with. Your skin, hair, eye color, and height—you didn't choose. You were born in the age of the internet, not the age of the Inquisition (be thankful for that). You also played no role whatsoever in choosing your parents, grandparents, aunts, uncles, and siblings (though you may indeed wish to swap some players in that fantasy league). All the basic well-being stats, such as your predicted lifetime income level, your education, health, religion, political party, and even whether or not you'll eat brussels sprouts, kale salad, and quinoa when you're forty—all of those can be determined almost entirely by your parents. Yikes. Most of us don't like to admit that. But the statistics show that who your parents are greatly influences who you will become.

Now, that news could be really exciting or it could be scary. You might even have mixed feelings. But take heart. This isn't some fatalistic predetermined path you have to follow. You can still blaze your own trail.

Take Jeff Kemp, for example. Jeff was born to an uber-successful, larger-than-life personality. His dad, Jack Kemp, was a pro quarterback, winning MVP awards and an AFL championship. He was popular in politics, serving on President Reagan's cabinet and even running for president and vice president. So Jeff was born in his dad's shadow (no pressure). But he adored his dad and tried to model his life after him. And like his dad, Jeff went on to have a career as a pro quarterback. But after eleven years in the NFL, Jeff didn't follow his dad into politics. Instead, he started a nonprofit ministry to strengthen families. He was like his dad in many ways, but he went his own way in others.

So yes, your family has a huge influence on the person you become. They open and sometimes close doors you might not have known existed. They shape your value system in huge ways, for good and sometimes for ill. And more than likely you will grow up to be like your parents in more ways than you know.

Culture

The culture you live in—the country, community, even ethnic culture—also has a big influence in shaping you. In fact, you often decide which feelings you're going to follow based on what the culture tells you. This is another one that's hard to accept. We want to believe we are in complete control of our decisions and directing our lives. But that really is an illusion. Not convinced?

I've heard Tim Keller, a pastor and author in New York City, describe it this way:

Imagine 1,200 years ago, [there's] an Anglo-Saxon warrior walking through the streets [of his village]. And he looks into his heart and sees a couple of deep feelings. One is aggression. He just loves smashing people. If someone gets in his way, he loves killing them. And he looks at himself and sees that aggressive impulse and he says, "That's me. I like that. I'm going to express that." On the other hand, he sees another feeling . . . he sees same-sex attraction. What's he going to say? "That's not me. Nope. We're going to squelch that."

[Now imagine] a young man walking down the street in Manhattan today. He looks into his heart and sees aggression. What's he going to say? "I need therapy. I need anger management." But [when] he looks in his heart [and] sees same-sex attraction, he says, "That's me."

What's going on here? The Anglo-Saxon's culture is based on [shame and] the idea that society will fall apart if it doesn't respect strength. So the best thing you can do for society if someone crosses you is to kill them. His culture was telling him that some feelings are really you and some are not. And our modern culture is doing the same.[1]

What is acceptable in one culture might not be in another, and you make daily decisions based on culture without even realizing it. It's like the old joke about a fish that meets a frog, and the frog says, "Gee, the water sure is nice today." And the fish says, "What water?" Once you stop laughing, I'll explain . . . Just like a fish isn't even aware of the water they swim in, your culture surrounds you, shapes you, moves and directs your life without your even being aware of it. So without realizing it, your culture tells you which feelings you should follow and which you should ignore.

Male and Female

The Bible starts with a family and ends with a family. And from the very beginning, God made one key distinction in the human race:

He created a man, and then He created a woman. Male and female. Two distinct sexes.[2] And that word *and* between "male and female" is all the difference between just one lonely dude hanging out with herds of hound dogs for hundreds of years and our entire civilization. Because without a woman, a man doesn't make more people. God had a design in creating two distinct sexes. And the way you are born has a huge influence on your identity. It shapes the way you think about yourself and the way you interact with your culture and the world. And it's not just perception and cultural influence. There are real scientific and biological differences between men and women. I'm going to paint in generalities here—there are exceptions—but statistically, everything that follows is true.

In general, men are stronger and taller and have more body hair than women. Women live longer, sing higher, and tend to have more babies (many more, in fact). Men are more aggressive, take more risks, get struck by lightning a lot more frequently than women,[3] and wreck their cars as often as an eighty-year-old, gray-haired grandma.[4] Women do a better job of nurturing and caring for those in need and tend to have a stronger sense of commitment. Men tend to be more analytical and compartmentalized while women tend to factor emotion and the big picture into decisions. Even the structure of the eyeball is different for men and women.[5] That's why kindergarten boys tend to color with one dark crayon, scribbling as furiously as possible, while girls pick every pastel shade in the carton to portray a pony prancing in a field of petunias.

These days there are lots of conversations about gender and how it gets expressed, which we'll talk more about later. But the point for now is that being born a boy or a girl shapes your identity in significant ways.

Friends

Your friends play a HUGE role in your identity formation. In fact, you're probably looking to your peers for a sense of identity now more than to your parents. Approval from your peers feels so important;

you're often more easily persuaded to do things you wouldn't normally do to gain their approval. And sometimes it's unexplainable. In high school I believed that having a Coca-Cola T-shirt, an L.L. Bean jacket, a Swatch watch, and a pair of Eastland shoes (worn without socks) would make me more popular or more important. I look back at that and just laugh (and if you search for pictures of this getup, you will too). At some point, you'll look back on whatever gives you street cred now and do the same. It's part of the reason why your friends might try drugs, steal things, have sex before marriage, watch porn, and even listen to classical music (gasp!) to gain the approval of others. It feels good when people like you, even if for the wrong reasons.

Here's the cool part, though. Friends can also positively shape you in a powerful way during this season. A friend came to me a couple years after high school and said, "The way you were always looking to be active and push yourself to learn, that really inspired me." In fact, after barely graduating high school and launching his career working part-time jobs and living with his mom, he decided that maybe another route would lead to more happiness in life. He got focused and went to college. This is a guy who almost didn't graduate because he missed fifty days of school his senior year just goofing off. Fifty! You never know how you might be influencing others for good without realizing it.

A well-known Bible teacher and motivational speaker, Charlie T. (as in "Tremendous") Jones, has a famous quote: "You'll be the same person tomorrow as you are today except for the books you read and the people you meet." You can be intentional to surround yourself with friends that push you to grow, but one thing is for sure—the people you spend the most time around will shape you, for better or for worse.

Books and Mentors

Reading great books about great people will change you. C. S. Lewis, Winston Churchill, Elisabeth Elliot, Margaret Thatcher, all had the course of their lives shaped from an early age by books. Former President Ronald Reagan listed one of his favorite books as *That Printer of Udell's*, which tells the story of Dick Falkner, who rises above his troubled past and becomes a godly man. When Reagan finished reading it as a young man, he told his mom, "I want to be like the guy in that book." In Falkner, he saw a man of character and integrity, and spent the rest of his life trying to live up to that standard.[6]

Books can serve as mentors in your life—but you also need to pursue real mentors. These are people older than you who can give you wisdom. Whether two years older or thirty, both have lots to offer. Having a mentor doesn't have to be a formal thing, but when you see someone you want to be like, do all you can to be around them. Our church youth group leader was a guy I looked up to and admired at so many levels. If he was leading a Bible study or leading a mission trip, I was there. There was no other place I wanted to be than around him. He was, and is still, a man of deep character. He shaped my life in many ways.

Many other things shape your identity: your successes in sports and in school, but also your failures, as well as your romantic relationships. (Man, those can really shape you. In fact, there's a whole chapter on this later.)

Here's the big point: There's not simply one defining characteristic that totally explains you to the world. Many things shaped your identity to form the awesome person you are today.

I hope this book will help you take hold of shaping your identity. Many folks just float down the river of life, waiting for whatever comes their way, drifting wherever the river leads. That can be great (I love a good float trip), but there are times you need to take charge of the journey, paddle yourself out of the river, and go somewhere else. This book is about giving you the vision, the courage, and the tools to do that.

And here's why. Because there's more to life than whatever seems ultimate right now. There really is. Many teens get trapped in a downward spiral, believing that the momentary praise of peers is what gives true meaning to life. Yes, there's always a chance the things your peers praise may be a really big part of the rest of your life. But there's a good chance you'll look back on your high school years and laugh till you cry at what seemed so critical to your happiness at the time.

So we're going to start with the one thing that will last: the key to finding a true identity. If you get this right, it will put everything else in perspective.

Make It Personal

- How would you describe yourself to others? What five words would you use?

- What areas do you feel give you a sense of identity (e.g., friends, hobbies, academics, music, church, family, work)?

- If you could change one thing about the person you are, what would it be? (It could be something you don't like and you want to get rid of, or something you would like to have that you don't currently have.)

2

The Ultimate Source of Identity

One night I was lying in bed, almost asleep, when I heard what sounded like an elephant stomping on a car-sized Coke can and dragging it off to the recycling center. There haven't been many elephant sightings in my neighborhood—nor are elephants known for being faithful recyclers—so I got up to inspect the situation. I looked outside and, instead of an aluminum can, there was a mangled car rolling away from the scene. The car had smashed my neighbor's treasured pickup truck parked in front of his house.

We lived on a normally quiet street—hardly any traffic (or elephants) in the evenings—so my guess was that the driver was highly intoxicated. And now the neighbor's truck looked like our environmentally friendly elephant had played hacky sack with its front end. Not pretty. But what happened next was what really stuck with me. I saw my neighbor, normally a calm and controlled guy, rush outside and completely lose it. He screamed like a wild gorilla that had just lost its firstborn, and ran off in hot pursuit of the car.

Now, I've been in car wrecks. It can be an emotional experience, especially if you or a loved one is injured. But I've never seen someone so rattled by a damaged vehicle. A car wreck is no fun. It's a hassle to get everything fixed or replaced, but it's not something that should completely unravel your world. If it does, you have to ask yourself, why was this vehicle so important? Why did this event send me off the deep end? Is my identity so fragile that a car wreck unravels it?

It's easy to point fingers, but I've come unglued over less significant things. The point here is to be able to endure hard times and set a course that is meaningful and fulfilling. And to do that, your identity has to be rooted in something stronger than yourself.

The popular idea today is that you have to look deep within yourself to discover your true identity. That is a scary thought. What if you don't like what you find? No, this course of action simply won't work. Why, you ask? Well, think of how many times you've let yourself down. You tell yourself, "I'll never do that again." And within forty-eight seconds you do it again. Or you tell yourself, "I'll always be a happy person." And then you get sad that you're not suddenly happy. None of us live up to our own expectations for ourselves, which is a bummer.

So you have a couple of options. One is to drop your expectations to such an abysmally low level that it becomes impossible to let yourself down. I had a friend like that. He would say, "My goal every day is to get out of bed. That way if I do anything beyond that, I feel like an overachiever. The reason why so many people walk around disappointed with themselves is that they set too high of expectations." Well, that's one approach.

But another is to find something outside of yourself that you can lean on for strength, for direction, for purpose. Something utterly dependable when you can't depend on yourself. Something that will hold up in every situation.

And that thing is actually a person—and His name is Jesus Christ.

Colossians 3:2–3 says, "Set your mind on things above, not on the things that are on earth. For you have died and your life is hidden with Christ in God."

When your identity becomes hidden, or rooted, in the revelation of who Jesus is and what He has done, rather than on what you find hidden deep inside yourself, you can live life to its truest, not distracted by whatever momentary messages are dictating the way you live. When you "hide" your identity in Christ, it's not hidden from others but protected by Christ.

I know this is a big concept. What does it mean to have your identity hidden in Christ? Do you get there by finding a catchy bumper sticker? Or maybe by writing "Jesus" on the organ donor line of your driver's license? Do you give Him the keys to your heart somehow?

Pastor Rick Warren, author of *The Purpose Driven Life*, one of the bestselling books of any kind in the last twenty years (over 30 *million* copies sold), says it means "That you abandon any image of yourself that is not from God. . . . You start believing what God says about you."[1]

Finding your identity in Christ means believing that what God says about you is truer than what anyone else (including yourself) says. When you're tempted to believe that you're either much better than you really are, or much worse than you really are, look to what the Bible says about you.

So what does the Bible say about your identity?

Well, it says a lot. Some good things. Some bad things. Let's start with the bad.

You—yes, adorable little you—were born full of sin. We all were. Of course, you were incredibly cute even ten seconds out of the womb, but you still were full of what a friend of mine calls P.U.S: pride, unbelief, and self-love. You wanted what you wanted, and that's all that mattered. This came to you because from the beginning of time, humankind has rejected God's plan (see Romans chapter 5). We could go on, but I think you get the point. It wasn't pretty.

However, for those who believe in Christ, the story takes an amazing turn.

I love to go to the book of Ephesians and look at all the places in the first chapter where it says "in Christ" or "in Him." Depending on your Bible translation, those phrases appear about eleven times and describe a host of incredible things about ourselves that if we *truly* believed, would change everything. It says that those in Christ are "blessed with every spiritual blessing in the heavenly places" (v. 3), chosen (v. 4), predestined and adopted (v. 5), redeemed and forgiven (v. 7), grace has been lavished on them (v. 7), that they are in the know on God's will (v. 9), have been given an inheritance (v. 11), and are sealed by the Holy Spirit (v. 13). Those are some weighty statements. Entire books have been written about the meaning and depth of each of those truths. You could spend the rest of your life dwelling on just one and still not come to fully grasp it.

If you come to base your identity in these statements—if you believe these words are one hundred million thousand times truer of you than anything else you might believe about yourself, it roots and hides your identity in something that can't be changed and can't go away.

So if you're a world-renowned guitar player and your fingers get chopped off in the latest smoothie-blender sensation, your identity doesn't crumble. If you become the finest pole-vaulter of your generation, and then blow out your knee playing shuffleboard, life is still meaningful because of who you are in Christ. And yes, even if your treasured truck gets destroyed in a stomp-and-run accident, you can still function. Life won't crumble.

Once your identity is rooted in Christ, how do you help Mom and Dad go along with the program? I mean, we all know that they're the big stumbling block to good times and happy days, right? No better way to kill a cool idea—like an overnight ski trip with your best buds—than to tell Mom and Dad about it. Yeah. Well, let's talk about that. . . .

3

Independence without Isolation

ndependence. We all want it. All of life is about growing in independence. As an infant, you completely depend on your parents for everything. Without them you'd have zero chance of survival. You don't remember a single diaper change, not a pound of pureed sweet potato shoveled into your mouth, nor any all-night crying sessions with your frazzled parent. But you wouldn't have made it without them.

Then things begin to change. You start to scoot, then crawl, then waddle through the house. You cruise from couch to chair, bringing the house down with claps of delight. And once your arms get long enough, you learn to yank off your clothes and sometimes put them back on. You even pick up a fork and put food in your own mouth. Yay you!

This keeps happening, and eventually you figure out most of the basic necessities of life. In fact, you're already there. If you had to, you could pretty much survive on your own. It might not be pretty. You might not flourish, but you could get the essentials done. And so now you're starting to feel that huge tension teens and parents encounter: your desire to be your own person—to be completely independent. To run your own life, rule your own roost, be in charge of your own destiny.

But how do you get there? I mean, your parents don't let you do just any and everything you want. So how do you help them get to the point where they will?

Let's start with a quick reality check. It's hard to believe that what you're about to read really is true, but here it goes: Your parents really do want you to be independent. They want you to be out on your own! Like I said, it might be hard to believe, but it's true. I PROMISE they do not want you living in their house the rest of your life, depending on them for money, cars, insurance, cell phones, pizza, rides to practices and games, clothes, gummy worms, paper, and protractors. No, they would eventually like to spend that money on something else, like a vacation to Europe this summer, or tap-dance lessons, or a new compound bow.

Now, here's the catch. The reason your parents don't let you do whatever you want is because they want you to find *successful* independence. If independence alone were the goal, they would have kicked you out of the house the day you were born. But then they'd be in prison. Even if you survived, it wouldn't have been very successful for you. They know their job is to help you grow into a person who doesn't just barely survive but flourishes. They don't do it perfectly—no parent does—but independence is their goal.

The key word is *successful* independence, but what does that mean? Well, to illustrate, I'm going to tell the story of everyone's favorite nineteenth-century missionary—my great, great, great uncle Emory Reese. He and his wife lived in eastern Africa for twenty-five years in the late 1800s and early 1900s. They worked to translate the Bible into a tribal language. They did it so well the regional government had them develop courses for the locals to learn to read and write their own language. Emory brought the first printing press to the area and developed one of the first brick factories, which, by his measure, produced the "finest bricks around."

Now, keep in mind this was an era when you left home for the mission field assuming you'd never come back. There were no eight-hour flights across the ocean to rescue you. No email or phone. Letters moved no faster than a train, horse, or boat. Many missionaries packed their belongings in a coffin so they'd have it with them to be buried in. Emory was thousands of miles and hundreds of hours from his parents back on the farm-speckled plains of Illinois. This was about as independent as you could get.

Early in his tenure as a missionary, Emory wrote a letter to his dad asking for advice, and his dad replied with this line: "Do the littles. Do them well and watch them multiply in thy hands." What he meant was, if you do the little things well and pay attention to detail, you'll see fruit eventually.

This is just a different way of saying what Luke 16:10 says: "One who is faithful in a very little is also faithful in much, and one who is dishonest in a very little is also dishonest in much" (ESV). This is probably the most helpful verse you can memorize and employ at this stage in life. If you want more freedom, prove you can handle the freedom you have already been given. I've often heard Dennis Rainey, an author, speaker, and the founder of FamilyLife, say, "The best measure of what a man can do is what he has done." Meaning, if you can't handle a very small responsibility, why would someone give you more responsibility? This holds true not just with your parents, but with your boss at work, your teachers, and even your friends.

Why is this so important? Because with increasing freedom comes increasing responsibility. You're not just being given more freedom for your own sake. No, almost always more freedom goes hand in hand with more responsibility. There's usually more risk, but also more reward.

When I was four I received my first bike. I remember seeing it under the Christmas tree, right next to the neon-green Oscar the Grouch puppet. That bike was like gold to me. The puppet was too, but I learned to love the bike. The tires didn't even inflate—they were just solid rubber—but I didn't care because it was the first taste of freedom. Well, freedom with training wheels. It took me a few years and a few scabs to get the hang of it, but once I did, I was off to the races. Some years later I upgraded to a BMX bike. Now I could go a lot faster and a lot farther. Mom made me check in every hour in the summers. So I pedaled as hard as I could for thirty minutes to get as far from home as possible, then turned around and did the same to get back home, check in, then repeat, over and over all summer. A little bigger taste of freedom! I could go farther, but I also got some bigger scrapes and ran into some trouble at times. Later, a ten-speed bike took me even farther, even faster. Then a motocross bike. Freedom kept growing.

But no bike compared at all to the speed and power of a car. Man, it was amazing how far from home I could get in a hurry. But the damage that can be done with a car is crazy compared to a bike. I mean, the worst that could happen on a bike, no matter how fast I barreled down the biggest hill, would be to seriously injure myself and maybe one other person if I plowed right into them. But with a car you can mess up an entire family, even buildings in a hurry. Just the other day I watched a neighbor's house have a boulder-sized hole covered over with brick because a car plowed through it in the night. *(Or was it an elephant?)*

With increasing freedom comes increasing responsibility. And if you want more freedom, show yourself to be trustworthy with the freedom and responsibility you've already been given.

Ask yourself this: What is one area in my life where I REALLY want more freedom right now? What's the first thing that comes to mind? Go ahead—write it down right here.

FREEDOM!: _____

Now that you know what it is, you can work with your mom and dad to move toward it instead of working against them. Go to them, tell them your desire, and ask them how you can work together to see it happen. You really can work together toward successful independence.

Three Keys to Successful Independence

There are three other things you'll need to move toward successful independence. And if you grasp these now, they'll serve you well the rest of your life. They're wisdom, relationships, and practice over time.

Wisdom

I once heard a well-known basketball player say, "Experience is the best teacher." Hmm . . . really? Experience is definitely *a* teacher, but if you only lean on experience to know how to live, you'll learn some hard lessons. In contrast, I love what Pastor Crawford Loritts says: "Experience is not always the best teacher, but it is the only school a fool will attend."[1] You can learn everything on your own, or you can learn from the mistakes and failures of others, which will take you further down the road. That is wisdom—learning from others. Mix that with your experiences and you'll be in a much better place to succeed.

But there's more to wisdom than just experiences. Dennis Rainey defines wisdom as "godly skill in everyday living." The key word being *godly*. To become wise, your wisdom has to be based in something greater than this world has to offer. Your own insight will only go as far as human experience. But true wisdom has to go deeper than that. Proverbs 1:7 says, "The fear of the Lord is the beginning of knowledge; fools despise wisdom and instruction" (ESV). Gaining true wisdom starts with fearing the Lord, with giving Him the respect and position He deserves in your life. That puts everything else in its proper place.

How do you find this kind of wisdom? Learn from the wise. Ask people you admire for insight when you're not sure what to do. Put yourself around those you want to be like. And hide God's Word in your heart. Psalm 119:11 says, "I have hidden your word in my heart that I might not sin against you" (NIV). Memorizing God's Word moves you toward wisdom because it shapes and transforms your mind—drawing you closer to His will and desires for your life.

My dad is one of the wisest men I know. God has definitely given him the gift of wisdom. I didn't always want to hear what he had to say, but I always listened (even if he didn't think so) because he modeled wisdom. He lived wisely, and underneath that wisdom was a dependence on the wisdom of God, not just his own intellect.

Relationships

A second thing you'll need to move toward successful independence is *relationships*. You can't become independent on your own. Sounds weird, but if you were completely independent from everyone, you'd be isolated.

In 1978, professor Buckley Crist walked into his office at Northwestern University, sat down at his desk, and started opening his mail. It was a stack of the usual stuff—letters, bills, some magazines and journals—but there was a suspicious package that caught his attention, so he called campus security. When the officer opened the package, a homemade pipe bomb exploded in his face.

That was one of sixteen packages delivered by what came to be known as the Unabomber. The manhunt for this evasive criminal was the most involved and costly investigation the FBI had ever undertaken to that point. Even with all this effort, after seventeen years, they had nothing. It was as if this person didn't exist. They were out of leads and at a dead end with the investigation. Then one day they got a call. "I think my brother might be the Unabomber. But I'm not sure. I haven't seen or spoken with him in six years." David loved his brother, Ted, but he wanted the bombings to stop. It was worth the risk to make sure.

Soon after, the FBI raided Ted Kaczynski's remote Montana cabin and found drafts of the Unabomber's writings, plans, and— the smoking gun—a fully assembled bomb ready to be mailed.

How did Ted—who grew up in a loving family, entered Harvard at age sixteen, was the youngest professor ever at UC–Berkeley;

a boy with a gentle spirit, who wouldn't pull the trigger rabbit hunting—end up as the Unabomber?

It's certainly a complex answer with a number of factors, maybe even some mental illness. But one thing that fed the problem was his isolation. Ted moved to the Montana wilderness and completely cut ties from his family. He excluded the people who could give him perspective, help him process, help him grow as an individual. He completely sealed himself off from the outside world. But the isolation didn't start in Montana. After entering Harvard at such a young age, he had struggled socially and began to isolate himself.

His brother, David, also moved to a remote ranch. His was in Texas, but he didn't seal himself off from the world. He went there for a season, to process some deeper issue in life, to better prepare himself to reconnect with the world. He eventually returned to society and married. David wanted to improve himself, while Ted was looking to retreat and retaliate, to punish the world he didn't understand.[2]

Independence is good, but *isolation* is a problem. You have to have people in your life you can trust that will help you grow and change and move toward healthy independence. When you're driving a car and you look in the mirrors, you can't see every part of the road. There could be a car right beside you but in your blind spot. Well, you've got blind spots in your life as well. You can either have people who don't like you point out your blind spots to everyone within shouting distance (that's the definition of junior high), or have the people who love and care about you point them out quietly and personally. Of course, the challenge comes in listening to those who say something difficult to hear. At first you'll want to get defensive and storm out of the room—but take a second and consider it. They may be right and it might help you grow. Besides, how are you going to see your own blind spots? It's not possible (thus the name "blind" spot).

I remember hanging out with a close friend when we were both about sixteen. We were at church one Saturday goofing around—just killing time waiting to play basketball with some friends. We started to play Ping-Pong, but I demanded that we follow *my* set of rules. He wanted to try something different. No way was I giving in. It was my way or the highway. Even though no one was watching, no scores were kept, no one else in the history of time cared one iota about that game, I wouldn't budge. He said forget it and walked away. I was a world-class control freak and couldn't see it, but when he stormed away, it shook me just a little. Why couldn't I be flexible just once? Why did I have to be in charge of every little thing? Would I want to hang out with a guy like that? No, sir. No way.

Your friends can play a huge role in helping you grow in character—so much so that we'll spend a good part of chapter 9 talking about how important friends are and how important it is to choose them wisely. But your parents, well, they'll always be your parents. You need to be strengthening that relationship as well so you can depend on them for years to come. But there are also coaches, mentors, teachers, pastors, neighbors, grandparents, aunts, uncles, brothers, and sisters. So many people can play an important role in helping you move toward successful independence.

Practice Over Time

One key to improving in any area of life is practice—repeating something over and over again and perfecting the finer movements until it becomes automatic.

Think about a hobby or skill or game you love to do and have become decent at. Did you get there magically? No, it came through practice. Even walking, though you don't remember it, came from lots and lots of practice. Driving is the same. Sports, music, art, they all require a significant amount of practice to become an expert in the field.

If you want to grow in independence, make sure to take time practicing and developing skills, because skills stick with you and serve you well your entire life. Sure, plenty of people have a natural talent and do okay with a minimal amount of practice, but no one becomes the best without lots of hard work.

I read an article recently about former NBA basketball player Kobe Bryant. Back when he was still playing professionally, a trainer was hired to travel with the USA basketball team to help the athletes prepare for the Olympics. One morning this trainer's phone rang at 4:15 a.m. It was Kobe. The trainer scrambled to meet him at the gym. By the time he arrived, Kobe was already drenched in sweat. Who knows how long he had been there. They did conditioning work for the next hour and fifteen minutes, then hit the weights for forty-five minutes. By then the trainer was toast. He went back to the hotel room and crashed. When he returned to the gym at eleven in the morning for the official team practice, Kobe was just finishing the shooting drills he started when the trainer left. Eight hundred makes was his goal, and he hit the last one as the guy walked in. Kobe, arguably one of the top five players of all time in the NBA, was working harder than anyone. You would think if anyone could coast at basketball, it would be Kobe. But he was still putting in the hard work.[3]

If you want to show yourself faithful in the little things, do what you can to get the wisdom you need from the people you admire, and put in the practice to get better. All that will help you move toward successful independence and help prepare you for the increased responsibility that goes hand in hand with increased freedoms.

SECTION 2

GENDER IDENTITY

WHAT DOES IT MEAN TO BE A MAN OR A WOMAN?

So far we've talked about all the different things that go into making up your identity. We've also talked about your desire to break off from your parents and become your own person—to live out that identity on your own.

The rest of this book is about the main areas where teens tend to struggle when wrestling with their identity. There are four main categories:

1. Gender Identity: What does it mean to be a man or a woman? And how do I know when I've become one?

2. Spiritual Identity: How do I make my faith my own—not just depend on the faith of my parents (whatever that may be) my whole life?

3. Relational Identity: How do I handle the relationships in my life (friends, peers, romantic interests) to help me succeed?

4. Missional Identity: What's my purpose? How do I figure out how God uniquely wired me to make a difference on this earth?

Let's start with manhood and womanhood.

Everyone wants and needs the answer to the question "What does it mean to be a real man or a real woman?" When I was in high school, I wanted nothing more than for others to call me a man. I started out in the JROTC (like a mini-Army-boot-camp program), and once a week we all dressed in our uniforms and had an inspection. Everything had to be perfectly pressed and polished; no room for sloppiness. But the one area that some guys avoided on purpose was shaving. There was no prouder moment than for the drill sergeant to announce to the entire group when, for the first time, a young man, who was a boy the day before, had lost points for not shaving. I was on the less-hairy side of my peers, so I never got that call. But it would have been a highlight of the year. It would have publicly announced my entry into manhood.

It's great being a little boy or a little girl. But life moves along and then it's time to grow up and become a man or a woman. But this isn't always obvious or easy. You may have been born clearly male or female, but it is less clear how one becomes a real man or real woman.

No one pops out of the womb pronouncing, "I'm the next Chuck Norris!" or "Watch out, Audrey Hepburn!" You don't even know what the words *boy* or *girl* mean for many years. And even then, those words and the way you live them out are shaped by a whole host of factors—like what your parents tell you is acceptable, what your friends praise or put down, or what your culture says is "manly" or "feminine." As a result, people can end up with some pretty weird definitions of manhood and womanhood.

I remember a friend telling me, "Real men don't put cream in their coffee." Really? What did cream ever do to become distinctly feminine? Is it because cows are all female? You know, I've seen plenty of manly men eat cream in a whole host of forms: whip cream, ice cream, Cream of Wheat (wait . . . I don't think that has cream in it). All those seem perfectly acceptable to men, but once cream touches coffee, you better push back from the coffee bar, mister, or else risk turning into a woman. That makes no sense (can you tell I like cream in my coffee?).

Conversely, I've walked the streets in Fiji where even the burliest dude might wear a skirt. It's part of their traditional cultural clothing. And they have some really tough guys. In fact, they usually have one of the top rugby teams in the world. It's a tiny island nation full of tough guys. In skirts.

Even in America, there were eras when leading men in politics and business wore wigs, girdles, lace, powder, and the equivalent of modern pantyhose. That was all acceptable at the time.

Sometimes preferences become rules, and when that happens, it makes everything weird—and hard to sort out what is essential and what is secondary.

So when it comes to really getting a handle on what it means to be a man or a woman, instead of getting caught up in the cultural chaos, you have to look to a standard. We're going to take a couple of chapters and try to unpack what the Bible says about manhood and womanhood. What really makes up the essence of what it means to be a man or a woman according to Scripture?

Once we've done that, we'll talk a little about gender identity. There's a ton of talk about the topic these days—and the conversation is changing rapidly. What should someone do if they have male parts but enjoy things that traditionally girls like? What if a boy would rather dress more like a girl? Or what if you have female parts but would rather play football than cheer? What do you do with all that? And even if you aren't wondering about this, how do you relate to friends who might be wrestling with these questions? Maybe you know someone who self-identifies as transgender. What does that mean? We'll explore all this as well.

Later in the book, when we talk about relationships, we'll dive into what you should do about your romantic attractions. What do you do if you find yourself attracted to someone of the same sex? What does the Bible say about it? How should you approach it, and how should you help others think about it? How do you relate to a friend who tells you they're gay, lesbian, bi, or some other title?

Light and easy subjects, right? Well, they're not the easiest topic for me to think about or write about either. I didn't even hear the word *lesbian* till seventh grade and didn't find out what it meant for a while after. But it's here and we can't stick our heads in the sand and pretend it will go away. You have to think about it and determine what you believe before you have to talk about it with others.

All right. First, let's talk about what the Bible says about manhood and womanhood. If you're a guy and you're reading this, go ahead and read the chapter for girls too. Same for you, girls. It's really helpful to know more about the opposite sex to help you understand and relate to them.

The Essence of Manhood

Every boy dreams of becoming a man. He stands before the mirror flexing his muscles, diligently studies his pits for the first signs of fuzz, measures himself next to his mom till he outgrows her, then next to his dad, relishing the day he might pass him as well. Body hair and muscle size are outward signs that a boy is becoming a man, but they certainly aren't the only measures of manhood.

So how do you know when you've become a man? And how do you learn what it means to be a *real* man? Well, there are many places to look: men's magazines, movies, TV shows, Twitter, sports stars . . . all of these have something to say about what makes a real man.

But with most all of these sources, the glaring omission is the chasm of content on the key components of *authentic* manhood: things like character development, investment in the next generation, leaving a lasting legacy, faithfulness, integrity, and fidelity. These traits all go unnoticed.

When does a boy become a man?

Check all that apply . . .

- ☐ getting first car
- ☐ getting a job
- ☐ graduating college
- ☐ getting married
- ☐ having kids
- ☐ finding his purpose in life
- ☐ moving out of his parents' house
- ☐ mentoring others

So in the midst of so much confusion about the definition of manhood, where does a boy turn to learn to be a real man?

Men Learn from Other Men

Boys become men by watching men, by standing close to men. Manhood is a ritual passed from generation to generation with precious few spoken instructions. Passing the torch of manhood is a fragile, tedious task. If the rite of passage is successfully completed, the boy-become-man is like an oak of hardwood character. His shade and influence will bless all those who are fortunate enough to lean on him and rest under his canopy.

—Preston Gillham[1]

When it comes to learning how to be a man, I hope you're looking to other men that you trust. You probably have some great examples with your dad, granddad, uncles, pastor, a coach, or one of your teachers. These are great guys to look to for wisdom and insight on manhood.

But maybe you don't have a dad around right now. Maybe he skipped town or passed away. Or maybe he's physically there but emotionally distant. And maybe there aren't many other men around you. That puts you in a challenging place, one that's hard for a lot of young men to overcome. But you need to know that God can still bring you good role models and help you grow into manhood. Whether your dad is around or not, know that no mere man can teach you *everything* you need to know about manhood. Ultimately we have to look to a perfect standard to get our definition of manhood.

First Corinthians 16:13–14 gives us a great starting place: "Be watchful, stand firm in the faith, act like men, be strong. Let all that you do be done in love" (ESV). There's a ton of great ideas in this verse. Just the fact that it says "act like men" tells us the Bible has expectations for how men should act.

So let's look at what the Bible says about manhood. To do that I'm going to unpack some things based on the book *Stepping Up* by Dennis Rainey. He says that there are five main stages, or steps, a man goes through in his life:

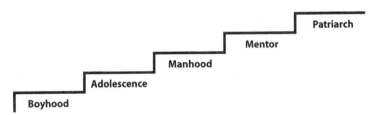

Dennis says one of the keys to manhood is to keep stepping up to each stage and to not get stuck on a step or try to straddle two steps. For instance, you don't want to keep one foot on the boyhood step while trying to move up to the manhood step. I've heard a guy like that called a "boy who shaves." This isn't one of those creepy bearded babies you might see at the state fair. No, he's someone who has a man's body but still acts like a boy in many areas of his life. A man keeps moving into new stages and trusting God to help him reach down to those who are on the step below them and help them step up as well.

Let's use that idea of "Stepping up" and put together a four-part definition for manhood. To STEP up to manhood, a boy should learn to S.T.E.P.

S: Stand firm

T: Take initiative

E: Engage others with wisdom and grace

P: Plan ahead and provide

Now, let's look at what each of these means.

S: Stand Firm

One phrase in 1 Corinthians 16:13 is "stand firm in the faith."
The bottom line is that men don't run away when things get tough. They are the ones that can be counted on. There's a story of Harry Truman, the thirty-third president, who was an artillery officer during World War I. During one of his unit's first battles along the border between France and Switzerland, they began firing upon the enemy across a valley. For some reason, though they were indeed at war, they did not expect the enemy would fire back. They were having loads of fun launching shell after shell for over half an hour. It was like the world's greatest Fourth of July party, but one thing was different: eventually, the other side did indeed fire back. And when those first shells began to explode around Harry and his crew, the soldiers scattered for cover, running away from their guns and posts. Almost everyone bailed except Harry—and he became famous for that incident, for standing firm in the face of fear when others were running away. (Of course, he later confessed in a letter to his wife that he was "too scared to run and that is pretty scared.")[2]

That incident defined Truman's life. He became known for being willing to do the hard thing when no one else would. Truman popularized the phrase "the buck stops here," embodying his sentiment: I'm not shirking away from the hard things, and I'll not pass them off to someone else.

Standing firm certainly means not running away when things get tough, but it also means knowing what you believe ("stand firm in the faith"). It's a quiet strength based on something stronger than yourself.

When my high school biology teacher made the case for evolution, I had a choice to make—was I going to stand for what I believe, or cave to his views? I humbly and respectfully disagreed, and was surprised to see him respond in kind. It was a good lesson that you can stand firm without being a jerk. You can still show respect for others and their views without putting them down. I've rarely won someone over (or been won over) through anger, arguments, and strife. It's usually the other way—someone presents a view out of kindness and humility, and over time I come to see their perspective and give it some thought. That's called wisdom. And you need much wisdom to know when to stand firm and when to flee.

There's no magic formula to know when to stand firm. Just look at the life of Paul in the book of Acts. There were times when he fled a city (Acts 9:23–25), but there were also times when he stayed around long enough to be beat like a piñata on Cinco de Mayo (Acts 14:19–21). How do you know when it's right to stay and face persecution, and when it's right to flee?

The key idea here is to stand firm in the faith. You need to know what you believe and what is worth standing for. A friend of mine, Bible teacher and author Alan Scholes, has a helpful distinction.[3] He says there are opinions, persuasions, and convictions. Opinions are matters you could give or take; you hold them, but not strongly. Persuasions are items you find important to you, and you value them strongly, but not so much that you would lose your job or house over.

Convictions are beliefs that are absolutely central to your life—so much so that you would even die over them. In order to stand firm, you need to know what your convictions are. You're going to have a lot fewer convictions in your life than persuasions or opinions. Convictions are what you want to make sure you stand firm for. But even then, there's still no magic formula. Every situation is a little different. The important thing is to seek wisdom and to know what's worth standing for.

Measure your ability to "Stand Firm" on a scale of 1 to 10, 1 being "wet noodle" and 10 being "Washington Monument."

1 2 3 4 5 6 7 8 9 10

T: Take Initiative

Probably one of the most defining aspects of manhood is taking initiative. A man doesn't wait around for others to do the hard work—he gets out in front and goes first when others are avoiding the hard things. He is a man of courage, one who is willing to do the right thing—the hard thing—no matter the cost.

If you want to know how a man will act in a tough situation, take note of how he handles less-challenging situations. It won't tell you everything, but it is something.

George Patton was one of the most famous generals of World War II. He even had tanks named after him. Now that's manly. Not even *Chuck Norris* has a tank named after him! Patton was known for being out front—pulling his troops along rather than pushing them from the back. He would tell young lieutenants, "Your troops are like a string of spaghetti—they can't be pushed from behind; you have to get out front and pull them along!" He was also known for being a man of action, saying, "A good plan violently [passionately] executed now is better than a perfect plan next week." He was a man of action in battle, and as a result, a man who saw many victories. But his action-first attitude didn't suddenly start when he became a general. Even as a plebe in his first year at West Point, others noticed this about him. He would go first when others declined. In one class, a professor displayed an induction coil with a twelve-inch spark. One student wondered if it was lethal to humans. Patton stuck his hand in it to find out and didn't even flinch.[4]

Now, going first isn't always the best route. Sometimes it's strategic to let others go first, especially if others have more skill and experience than you. But the question is, do you have an attitude of initiative? Are you willing to go first or do the hard thing when most would rather crash out on the couch to watch TV and eat cheese curls?

One thing I loved to do in high school was go on backpacking trips. My dad and I went at times, but I also went with a couple of men at church who led trips for a Boy Scout–like organization called Royal Ambassadors. One time we went to Cumberland Falls in central Kentucky, a truly amazing place. It's one of the few places on earth that has a moonbow. That's not some kind of weird haircut your dad sported in the '80s; it's a rainbow that you can see at night in the moonlight. Amazing.

We were there hiking around one of the smaller waterfalls that feeds into the Cumberland River. We were scrambling from one sunbaked boulder to the next at the base of the waterfall, trying to avoid slipping into the deep pools around us. Next thing I knew, I hear splashing and gurgling. This wasn't the playful kind of splashing, nor the gurgling of a pure mountain spring. These were the sounds of a boy doing his best not to drown. And there I stood, frozen in time, watching him flounder, trying to figure out what was happening. At that moment I felt something whoosh past me, bounding from rock to rock like Usain Bolt on a mountain goat. Within a couple of nanoseconds, Phil, our group leader, was launching himself into the water. Before I could even blink, he was already dragging the boy out, having saved his life. I still remember Phil standing there in all his clothes, sopping wet, putting his water-logged hat back on and pulling out his wallet to make sure he still had it.

The thing that stood out to me that day was the huge difference between a boy and a man. While us boys were standing and watching, trying to figure out what was happening, Phil, a man, took action. He didn't even take his wallet out of his pocket. A man takes action while boys stand around. A man is alert to the situation and aware that something could go wrong and is on guard, ready to act when needed.

Don't be like Saul, who though he had the appearance of a man, hid behind a stack of suitcases when he was asked to lead a nation (see 1 Samuel 10). Take the initiative; don't hide from responsibility.

Measure your ability to "Take Initiative" on a scale of 1 to 10, with 1 being "jellyfish" and 10 being "Navy Seal."

1 2 3 4 5 6 7 8 9 10

E: Engage Others with Wisdom and Grace

One way to tell the difference between a man and a boy is to see how he treats those weaker than he is. Does he use a position of power to take advantage of others, or to serve others? A real man knows how to engage others with wisdom and grace. He knows not to be domineering with his strength, but to use it to make others better.

Some men never figure this out. They think they are the center of the universe. They were tyrants as toddlers, and they take that same terrible attitude into marriage. They read the verse in the Bible that says "the husband is the head of the wife" (Ephesians 5:23) and take it to mean they have biblical permission to stomp all over their family. But they fail to keep reading to where it says "husbands, love your wives, just as Christ also loved the church and gave himself up for her" (Ephesians 5:25). Jesus, who was the very source of strength for the church, willingly gave up His life on behalf of the church. He knew how to engage others in a way that made them better.

How about you? Do people love being around you because you make them better? Or do they cringe when they see you coming?

There's a guy that I pray to be like when I grow up: Chuck Farneth. He is truly one of the manliest men I have ever met. He grew up working on the rivers around Pittsburgh, running tow-boats, tossing around big bull ropes lashing barges together. He has forearms like Wolverine and a smile as wide as the Mississippi River. Chuck is most known now for his abilities as a fly-fisherman, even winning a gold medal in the ESPN outdoor games. But here's the thing about Chuck: Even though he's one of the best in the world at what he does, after spending five minutes with him, you'll think *you* are one of the best in the world. He doesn't need to stroke his own ego; he's always seeking to build up others and make them better. That's the kind of guy I want to be like.

I've often heard it said that if a young lady wants to know how a young man will treat her, she should look at how he treats his mom and/or his sisters. If he's cruel, domineering, rough, or crass with them, that's a bad sign. But if he shows respect, if he's courteous, if he seeks to serve the women in his life, if he puts their needs before his own, that's a good sign that he'll do the same with his wife.

So start now, learning how to treat others in a way that engages them with wisdom and grace. Don't be a bully. Don't use your strength to "Lord it over" others (Matthew 20:25). Instead, learn to treat your mom/sisters with kindness. First Corinthians 16:13–14 says to "be strong," and the true measure of strength is how you treat those who are weaker than you.

> Measure your ability to "Engage with Wisdom and Grace" on a scale of 1 to 10, with 1 being "bull-in-china-shop" and 10 being "ballet dancer."
>
> 1   2   3   4   5   6   7   8   9   10

P: Plan Ahead and Provide

Most American men have it stuck in their head that "provision" is primarily about money. They think if you're a good provider, your kids can go to private school, spend a week on the beach in the summer, go on their senior class trip to Europe, and attend whatever college they want. Now, financial provision is certainly important, but that's the *result* of being a provider, not the purpose.

Former Green Beret Stu Weber tells the story of the Old West scout—the man whose job was to get out ahead of the wagon train and see if there were any dangers lurking ahead. He might find a bridge out, or a pack of wolves, or a merry band of miscreants waiting to ambush the train. Whatever it was, his job was to identify the danger and come up with a plan to avoid it.

Stu says that the word *provision* can be broken into two parts: "pro" and "vision." The *vision* part means "to see"—to take notice of what is going on around you; to be aware of the surroundings. The *pro* part means "before" or "ahead." Get out ahead of others and see what's happening before it causes problems. "Pro-vision" is thus "seeing ahead." That's a great picture of what it means to provide.

Years ago I worked as an assistant for Dennis Rainey, whom I've mentioned before. He was a mentor to me, and I wanted to learn all I could from him. The job wasn't very glamorous—lots of little tasks that freed him to focus on the work he could do best. One of the first things he said about the job was, "You need to get out ahead of me." I didn't know what that meant at first, but I quickly realized he was talking about pro-vision. He would explain, "Get out ahead of me and see if there are any problems you can solve before I even know about them." My job was to eliminate issues before he even knew they existed. Kind of like a hit man for problems. Except not very dangerous. Or illegal. That job taught me a powerful lesson: A man serves by eliminating problems before others even know they exist. He gets out ahead of his family and his friends, and serves them with a quiet strength.

I recently read a story about a thirteen-year-old boy who had already started building a house. His family lives on an old farm with lots of acreage. He asked his dad if he might start building his own house on a corner of the property so that he could start planning to provide for his wife someday. He takes whatever money he makes and, instead of spending it on video games, he buys building supplies. His dad helps out when he can, but this is primarily his son's project. Wow—now that's pro-vision. That young man is seeing out *way* ahead of most. I couldn't have even thought about marriage at thirteen—that seemed *so* far off, and it was, and should have been. The point is that we're all called to be looking ahead for the needs of others we care about.

When the Bible says "be watchful" in 1 Corinthians 16:13–14, it's talking about pro-vision. It's talking about an intentionality of character that says, "I will get out ahead of others and serve them by putting them first, rather than myself."

Measure your ability to "Plan Ahead and Provide" on a scale of 1 to 10, with 1 being "Mr. Las Vegas" and 10 being "Mr. Savings Account."

1 2 3 4 5 6 7 8 9 10

So that's one way to look at manhood from a biblical perspective. Real men S.T.E.P. up. They stand firm, take initiative, engage with wisdom and grace, and plan ahead and provide. And they do all this in love, not in a self-serving egotistical way but in a way that puts others first like Christ did.

When I was a boy, I looked to my youth minister at church, Kerry Jones, with great admiration. I learned more about authentic manhood from him than anyone else apart from my dad.

Kerry had all the stereotypical manly attributes: He was great at sports, was a weightlifter, had a beautiful wife and family—but he was also artistic. He could sing and play piano and guitar. And he led worship at church. But what meant the most to me was his strength of character. He is the only person I've ever seen calm a crowd of rabid seventh-graders with silence. His presence was so commanding that when he stood still, others grew quiet in anticipation of what he might say. He was full of wisdom because God's Word was always on his lips. He was constantly quoting Scripture; it seemed he had the entire Bible memorized. He was always charging us to pursue purity. He must have said a thousand

times, "Don't sacrifice the permanent on the altar of the immediate." He called us to a higher standard, and he did it in love. I
often prayed to be like him one day. And though we live hundreds
of miles apart today, I still relish any time around him.

There are lots of ideas floating around these days about what
it means to be a man. But the best place for you to look is to the
timeless standard of Scripture and the men around you who live out
the teachings of the Bible. This is supremely countercultural, but
it is the difference between boys who *look* like men, and real men.

5

The Essence of Womanhood

So what does it mean to be a woman in today's world? Does one become more of a woman with each baby born? Having children is certainly one aspect of womanhood, but is it the *ultimate* measure? Maybe not, since Eve, the first woman, was created fully woman before she ever had a child. Okay then, what else? Is it success? Is Oprah the ultimate woman? Or Beyoncé? Maybe Michelle Obama? Or is it more about looks? Name the most recent supermodel—is she the ultimate woman?

If you had to write out a definition of true womanhood—something that summed up the very essence of what it means to be a woman—what would you write?

Write out five words that mean "womanhood" to you
* _____
* _____
* _____
* _____
* _____

Not easy, is it? I think most young women are caught off guard by how difficult it is to put words to this. So, if you don't know what a woman should be, how can you expect to end up becoming one?

To figure out what's really at the core of biblical womanhood, we talked with a host of well-respected women. The thing we kept hearing over and over again was that you have to go back to the Bible to find a timeless standard for womanhood, because even the last fifty years has seen a huge swing in how people define womanhood. So we can't just assume that yesteryear was better than today. Instead, we need to look for a timeless definition based on a timeless standard.

A verse that guided the thinking on this topic is Proverbs 31:30: "Charm is deceitful and beauty is vain, but a woman who fears the Lord, she shall be praised." This verse helps take the conversation about womanhood off the temporary. The things of this earth—charm, beauty—are heavily worshiped in our world today, but they will pass away. However, the fear of the Lord (giving Him the proper respect and position He deserves) is something that will last. It drives at a lasting beauty based in an eternal standard, not just a momentary trend or fad.

We'll keep coming back to this concept over and over again throughout this chapter in an attempt to really root our definition of womanhood in God's Word.

If you're not so sure about the Bible being a trustworthy standard for something like this, just hear us out. Read what we've said about womanhood below and see if it makes sense. I think you'll find that the Bible is more relevant to this conversation today than you might have guessed.

One of the women I serve with at FamilyLife studied everything she could find on the topic of womanhood. She talked to many well-respected women who know the Bible and have taught on womanhood. She took everything she learned and boiled it all down to four main characteristics of biblical womanhood:

1. Holy beauty
2. Heart of a helper

3. Life-giver

4. Eternal focus

Holy Beauty

The desire to be beautiful starts at a young age for most girls. They put on Mom's makeup. They prance around in princess dresses seeking approval from Dad. And as they get older, they become more and more concerned with appearances and what other people think. On one level, it's a good thing to look nice and stay fit, but your outward appearance is not the whole picture of who you are. In fact, it's not even the most important part.

Yes, we live in a world that has made looks more important than character. But author and Bible teacher Leslie Ludy points out that our culture misshapes what starts as a good thing. "Women have that intrinsic desire to be found beautiful," she says. "We grow up wanting to be Cinderella and Sleeping Beauty, and the culture really preys upon that desire and warps and twists this good desire into something that is truly unattainable."[1]

It didn't always used to be this way, though. Other cultures and other times have elevated character over appearance. Remember Proverbs 31:30? "Charm is deceitful, beauty is vain. But a woman who fears the Lord is to be praised." Imagine what the world would be like if a woman's fear (of the Lord) factor was more highly esteemed than her beauty. How different would our world be?

We've been told that physical beauty is the ultimate beauty, yet physical beauty fades. Always. And if your significance is wrapped up in your outward appearance, it's only a matter of time until your world comes crashing down. Your beauty also has to be rooted in a beauty that is poured out into the lives of others—a beauty that isn't just focused on self, but on others.

Think about it: When have you been the least happy in life? When have you had the lowest amount of joy and sense of self-worth? Go ahead and see if you can think of a time. My guess is that it was likely a season when you were really focused on yourself. Numero uno. But thinking too much about yourself is a terrible place to be. You'll always end up down in the dumps when you do that. Turning your thoughts to the needs of others, which comes from an inner beauty, makes a huge difference in this world.

How does that happen? Leslie Ludy says, "Real feminine beauty comes from a life surrendered to Jesus Christ where his beauty shines through you; a selfless, poured out life."[2] There are a couple of great verses that can help us see what gives a woman holy beauty. Look at some of the characteristics here:

> Your beauty should not consist of outward things like elaborate hairstyles and the wearing of gold ornaments or fine clothes. Instead, it should consist of what is inside the heart with the imperishable quality of a gentle and quiet spirit, which is very valuable in God's eyes.
>
> 1 Peter 3:3–4 (HCSB)

Nancy DeMoss Wolgemuth, who teaches and writes books to women through her Revive Our Hearts ministry, explains, "To have a gentle and quiet spirit means we're not demanding. We don't insist on getting our own way. We trust in the Lord. She doesn't have to manipulate circumstances, or try to be in control of everyone around her. A woman with this kind of heart is a grateful woman. She blesses the Lord and others around her."[3]

Think of some of your friends. Do you know any who are demanding? Maybe they have to have things their way and can never be pleased. Maybe you're even that way at times. I know I have been.

But let's think of the opposite. Who do you know that is gentle, kind, thinking of others, not demanding, doesn't always have to be in control? They're often seeking your interest over their own. Who doesn't want to be around that kind of person!

The hard part is that these qualities aren't natural. They don't just suddenly appear. *"Man, I was walking around, and then bam, I just became completely selfless, totally focused on the needs of others."* Not happening that way. Instead, you have to pray for these qualities; you have to be intentional to develop them. You have to spend even more time fostering your internal beauty, your character, than you do your external beauty.

Think about how much time you spend to make yourself look beautiful. Instead of focusing on external beauty—hair and makeup and clothes—the Bible exhorts young women to develop an internal beauty, because that's the one that will not fade.

I've known of some young women that were so focused on their outward beauty—on their body image—that it became dangerous, and even deadly. So this is where we want to give you some warning and maybe some help.

Eating Disorders

Some girls become obsessed with dropping a dress size, getting thinner arms, or achieving skinny thighs. They so desperately want to be just a bit more "perfect" that they're willing to do almost anything.

But your efforts to find that "perfect" body can actually permanently damage your external beauty. I know of one girl who threw up so often to lose weight, her stomach acid ate away the enamel on her teeth. Now, as a young woman, she has false teeth. False teeth! Going to extremes to lose weight and find the "perfect body" can actually do the opposite.

Skipping meals will also cause low energy and headaches, among other potential physical issues. When you don't feel well, it's hard to really engage with other people. It's hard to focus. You just don't have the energy or the time to put effort into anything else. You'll need lots of energy in this stage of life to play sports, or dance, or learn an instrument, or develop or build on any new skills.

Bad breath is another side effect of skipping meals or vomiting to control weight. That's right, too much fasting will leave you with funk mouth. The last thing you want is for your breath to remind a friend of their socks after soccer practice. Eww.

The point is, starving yourself to become "beautiful" can actually cause harm to your beauty and health and your relationships and your future. It won't bring you the kind of happiness you seek; instead, it will do the opposite.

Now, I know you've heard some or all of this. Every school in the country has programs warning you of these dangers. So here's something I want to give you that they may not. What's way more important than being scared about the health risks of eating disorders? What's a thousand times more important is to come to believe the deeper truth that *there's so much more to you than your external beauty.* There really is. You're not just the sum of your body parts.

Listen to what the Bible says is true of you: "I praise you because I am fearfully and wonderfully made" (Psalm 139:14 NIV). *You* are fearfully and wonderfully made. And *fearfully* doesn't mean you'll scare people with your looks; it's like another way of saying "wonderfully." You were made with care and purpose.

You are beautiful. You may not fully believe that, but you are.

I have a daughter who's much younger than you, but every time I look at her I think of how beautiful she is. I am completely in love with her and so grateful she is my little girl. She just makes me smile. And I don't care how skinny or short or tall she is. All I care about is that she lives life to the fullest and falls more in love with Jesus every day. And I pray she would experience the deep satisfaction that comes from rooting her identity in Christ.

When I hear stories of girls really struggling with body image issues, and hear about some of the things they'll do to try and change their bodies, I think of my daughter and how much my heart would break for her if she were struggling in this way. I'd just want to hold her and tell her over and over again, "I love you, I love you, I love you. You don't have to do that to have real love. I LOVE YOU SO MUCH." I'd hold her and cry with her for days on end if it would help her. I want her to find rest in my love for her—and ultimately, God's love for her.

You may not have a dad in your life who would do that. Maybe he's not around, or maybe he passed away. He may even be causing some of your questions about your body image, but I can tell you with great confidence that God loves you deeply and cares so much more about you than your weight or body mass index or dress size. Those are not the best measures of your worth or significance. So keep dwelling on the truth that you are beautiful. God created you beautiful. Don't measure yourself by any other standard. If you're trying to match up to the images that are plastered all over our world, you're shooting for a fake standard. Even supermodels have come clean on how much of their appearance is faked. Photos are cropped and airbrushed, bodies are nipped and tucked. This is not reality.

> A fashion queen mannequin is taller than the average British man but with the waist of a 10-year-old girl.
>
> —M. G. Zimeta[4]

As you think more and more about the truth that God loves you, try to dig into the deeper issue—the root issue behind *why* you might be wrestling with this. Ask yourself some of the hard questions. Why would your weight or clothing size become the single most important thing in your life, so much so that you would sacrifice your health? Why would you be willing to make that kind of sacrifice? What is it you *really* want? Is it approval? Control? Attention? For others to like you? Do you miss feeling small as a child and are trying to revitalize the feeling of being a little girl? Are you living with a past hurt? Maybe it was something someone said or did to you that is driving you toward this behavior. Ask yourself these questions. Try to find out what is *driving* you so that it no longer has to *define* you.

For every five girls, one is battling an eating disorder, and will probably do so for many years. So more than likely you know someone who is dealing with this. If so, I can't encourage you enough to talk with someone about it. Get help, and get it soon. Don't wait.

The most beautiful people I know, the ones I really want to spend time with, are those who radiate beauty from the inside. They're great to be around because they give life to others, make them better, and almost seem to have forgotten about themselves. Those are the kind of people I want to be like, and the crazy part is that their attractiveness really has nothing at all to do with their physical appearance.

Pursuing your relationship with Jesus, making Him the center of everything in your life, that's the starting point for real holy beauty.

On a scale of 1 to 10, how tempted are you to base your sense of self-worth on your physical appearance?

1   2   3   4   5   6   7   8   9   10

Heart of a Helper

The Lord God said, "It is not good for the man to be alone; I will make him a helper suitable for him."

Genesis 2:18

That word *helper* can sound second-class, right? Well, it's not. Pastor and seminary professor Russell Moore says, "Sometimes when people hear that word helper, they hear 'assistant,' or, [they think it means] the man is doing the really important stuff and that the woman is simply helping him to do that."

I'm not sure why people have come to view this word that way, but many have. But here's the crazy part that Dr. Moore explains. "Helper" actually means the opposite of this.

The fact that God says "I will make a helper" for the man, [that's] saying he was deficient to do it all by himself. . . . Both of them are called to rule and to reign over the universe. In some ways they do that differently, but both of them are heirs of the universe. [She is not] "human-being junior." Everything that it means to be in the image of God belongs to her, and she has been given this task and this vocation.[5]

The Bible even refers to the Holy Spirit as a helper (John 14:26). So all along, God's plan was that His work would be accomplished by not just one, but two. The man desperately needed someone else to help him accomplish the work God had set out for mankind. They are meant to do this together.

So what is the work? At the very beginning of the Bible, in the first chapter of Genesis, you see the following:

1. Be fruitful and multiply
2. Watch over, care for, and govern the earth

Two pretty clear tasks. Start a family, and take care of the earth. And Adam and Eve were given this to do together. But it wasn't just about the task. It wasn't just about them getting things done. God also designed things this way for a greater purpose. Think about it—He could have just kept it simple with only Adam hanging out with the animals for all eternity. One guy equals fewer problems. With just one guy, there's no "flooding the earth" episode necessary, no plagues raining down on the Egyptians, no crazy wars and walls tumbling down. Who really wants all that mess?

Russell Moore explains:

> [God] did this so that He could point us to something even greater. God is one God, yet He also exists in three persons: God the Father, God the Son, and God the Holy Spirit. They all three exist together in perfect harmony and relationship for all eternity. They all have equal value, equal dignity, and equal worth. But they all have different roles to play in accomplishing God's purposes. And the same is true for us as men and women. We're equal in our value, dignity, and worth, but God made us with different strengths and different responsibilities, and called us to work together, using our differences to accomplish His purposes.[6]

Weighty stuff. A man and a woman, working together to accomplish God's purposes on earth, get and give a little taste of the Trinity when they're doing it the right way. Crazy. And when you, as a young woman, are living out your role as a helper, you're getting a taste of the Trinity in your life too.

Okay, so what do you do with this information right now, at your age? I mean, you probably don't live in a garden, and certainly not THE garden. And I suspect you're not married or "multiplying" yet. So what does it mean for a young woman your age to be a helper?

For this we interviewed Barbara Rainey. She has four daughters and helped start FamilyLife, a marriage and family ministry, in which she has served with her husband, Dennis, for over forty years. She had this to say:

> I think the most important thing a young woman can do is really focus on becoming the woman God created her to be. She's got gifts and talents and abilities that no one else on the planet has. So she needs to nurture those, and at the same time be growing and developing her relationship with God. She is developing a confidence in who she is as a person.
>
> How you relate to guys is just one part of how you live out this idea of helping. But there are many other ways, as well—like helping your friends make good choices, helping by being a role model to younger people in your life, helping older people by caring for them in times of need, or maybe comforting those who are grieving or healing from emotional or physical pain. But the point is that a godly woman will demonstrate a helping heart.[7]

Great ideas here on how you can practice the art of "helping" right now, as a young single woman. And I think you'll be amazed how others take note when you are intentional to help others.

This was one of the first things I noticed about my wife. And it was one of the main things that attracted me to her. Yes, of course I thought she was cute. I saw her curly blond hair across the room and thought, *I've got to meet that girl!* But then I noticed her character—how much she went out of the way to serve others time and again, to draw them into conversation, to focus on their needs rather than her own. She was thinking of others when I was only thinking of myself. And I thought, *I've got to get more time around this girl. I want to be like her.* Most of the girls I had dated up to this point, even some of the Christian girls at church, thought more about themselves and meeting their own needs than helping and serving others—so she really stood out as different.

So that is the second attribute of a godly woman—she has the "heart of a helper." God built that characteristic into the very creation of the woman. There's tons more that could be said about it, but for now you get some of the picture.

Here's the third attribute. . . .

Life-Giver

We asked some women, "Who is the ultimate woman?" And we heard the obvious names—the pop singers, politicians, actors, the famous-for-being-famous people. But there were also many who connected womanhood with being a mom. Women like Susanna Wesley, the Mother of Methodism, who had nineteen children. Some women mentioned their grandmothers, and many mentioned their own mothers and other mothers they knew and admired, like Barbara Rainey.

Obviously, moms are life-givers—they quite literally give life to everyone who ever existed. Your mom brought you into this world, or she adopted you to care for you, to sustain your life. (In fact, take a quick second to go find her and give her a big hug or drop her a thank-you note.)

Without a doubt, having babies is a pretty important job for women. But there's much more to being a life-giver than just *making* a baby. If you don't *care* for that baby—that new person—she won't last very long. You have to continue to give and sustain her life after birth. Think about all the things your mom does to make your life possible. She might encourage you when you're down, help you through disappointments and problems, cheer for you, and go out of her way to find what's best for you. That's all part of what life-giving means. She doesn't just want to see you barely survive—she wants to see you be your best. Not every mom does it well. In fact, some wish they could do a lot of things over. But they would agree there's more to "life-giving" than labor and delivery.

So you've got to be wondering again, *How can I be a life-giver right now, if I've not given birth yet?* Barbara Rainey has some great ideas on this too:

> Any time you speak positive words that are encouraging, that gives life to people. Think about your strengths. What are you best at? Are you an encourager who loves to be around people and build them up, or are you someone who wants to do something? You could teach a Sunday school class and pour into others that way, or sit with someone new at lunch and get to know them and give life to them. Or maybe do hair and nails at a nursing home. Writing thank-you notes is a life-giving activity because it honors a person for something they did. Also writing letters to encourage missionaries, or helping with sports programs in your community. Being engaged with people is what this is really all about, because if you are paying attention to others and not just thinking about yourself, which we're all prone to do, that's a big part of giving life. That's what Jesus did for us. He gave us life.[8]

God has put the desire and ability to be a life-giver at some level in the heart of every woman. For some, it's about encouraging and serving others. Some love to give life through creativity, painting, sewing, cooking, crafts; taking raw materials and making something complex and beautiful. Doing these things imitates God and His creativity.

Others give life by investing in children. Even before you have your own children, you can invest in the lives of other children. I knew a young lady named Abby. She grew up in the western United States but moved to Uganda after high school to help young boys who had been tossed out of their homes and were living on the streets. She helped serve at a home where they taught boys during the day, and offered help for life outside of school. She became like an older sister to many of those boys. She eventually married

Ideas for Life-Giving

Check ways that describe how you like giving life to others:
- ☐ Speaking positive words
- ☐ Helping with tasks
- ☐ Encouraging others
- ☐ Serving others
- ☐ Teaching a Sunday school class
- ☐ Sitting with someone new at lunch
- ☐ Serving at a nursing home
- ☐ Writing thank-you notes
- ☐ Writing letters to encourage missionaries
- ☐ Helping with community sports programs

a Ugandan man. Together they run the home that serves so many of these young boys, helping them become men, who wouldn't have a chance otherwise.

But you don't have to move to Uganda to give life to others. In fact, let's make it real. Think of one person who really drains the life out of you. When they are around, you can feel the fun getting sucked right out of the room. What can you do to give life to that person? They probably aren't happy that they have become the designated party-pooper. They probably don't want to stay that way. Or maybe they are normally a great person and have just rubbed you the wrong way. Shoot—they may even be a family member. Just take a second and think of one thing you can do to give life to them. Write it down. And do it this week. Don't wait!

I remember having a bad week in school one time. I had done poorly on a test and a big project and was starting to feel like I couldn't do anything right. But one day I showed up for class and one of the girls in class had bought me a new shirt. It was a little gift (and she was just a friend, so she wasn't trying to get my romantic attention). But she saw that I was having a hard week and wanted to brighten my day a little—to give life to me. And it really was a huge encouragement.

Life-giving is who you are. It's how you were wired. It's how God created you to be as a woman. It's part of your femininity. Even if you never get married or have children. Being a mother doesn't make you more of a woman, but it is a strong expression of the life-giving aspect of womanhood. Ask God to give you wisdom to practice giving life to others in this stage of your life.

So that's our third area: life-giver. We've got one more attribute of a godly woman to cover. But before we jump into that fourth one, I want to point out how there's a ton of overlap between these attributes. You probably noticed this—that these are all interconnected. Like how one of the ways *holy beauty* is revealed is by helping others, and how *life-giving* is just one aspect of how we love and serve others. They're all intertwined. This is important because life isn't just about coming up with a list of four separate categories that define you. Life is more complex than that. And how you live in one area affects the other areas, even if it's not always obvious.

Eternal Focus

This last attribute isn't unique to women. Guys need to have an eternal focus too. But we're including it here to emphasize how important it is for women to think about the big picture of life. What's my role in the world and what's my life supposed to be about?

Pastor and author John Piper believes that even though this is a huge question, young women can start thinking about it right now. "Young people are making incredibly important choices early on," he says. "I think they are eager and ready to hear someone call them to a radical kind of life that has a significance about it that is eternal and deep. So it seems to me that those who have any sense of reality at all know that if Christianity is real, then it's worth dying for. If it's not real, then let's not even talk about it."[9]

John Piper wants you to believe that life is about something much greater than yourself, much greater than all the little things we do every day. And if you can get that in your head and heart right now, it will make all the difference. It sure did for him.

He remembers the night his dad, a traveling evangelist, came home from a ministry trip and told a story that changed the way John thought about the future.

> With tears in [my dad's] eyes, he said, "A man came to Christ who must have been in his 70s. He'd been a sinner in the community for years and people had prayed for him and he'd resisted the gospel. And he walked to the front and he sat down, and after the service as I sat beside him, he just wept and wept. When I asked why he was weeping he said, and he repeated it over and over, 'I've wasted it. I've wasted it.'"

John continues to explain the meaning this story had for him. "Now, as a teenager, that story from my father landed on me with such power that I thought, *Never, ever, ever do I want to be able to say that I've wasted it.* From then on I had this impulse in me: 'Don't waste it, don't waste it!'"[10]

When you live life with an eternal focus, you live on purpose. You intentionally share Christ with others, and when you're doing that, you won't waste your life.

So what does this look like as a teenager? How do you live your life with an eternal focus? Let me introduce you to a young woman your age named Natasha Bray. Natasha's story has inspired thousands and thousands of her friends and fellow countrymen to live their life to the fullest, to live life with an eternal focus.

Natasha's story starts in New Zealand.

If you've never been there, it's a majestic place. Massive green mountains rise thousands of feet right out of the beach. Rolling inland hills spill out for miles in front of you and seem to sway like ocean waves. If you've seen *The Hobbit* or *The Lord of the Rings* movies, you get a picture of the country's beauty, since that's where they were filmed.

Natasha lived in Auckland, one of the major cities. She had blond hair, a quick smile, an adventurous spirit. She loved the outdoors and always had time to listen to her friends' struggles. She was quick to encourage, wanted to make the world a better place, and tried to make the most of every opportunity. She really had that kind of eternal focus we are talking about.

Her dad noticed this about her too. "She had a maturity of faith at a young age that I haven't ever seen again. I would take her out for breakfast Bible studies and she would do it with such enthusiasm." Dad might be a little biased, so what about a sibling? Olivia, her younger sister, admired her heavenly focus as well, saying, "She always had a genuine relationship with God that I wanted to follow and have for myself. She'd always be reading her Bible and teaching us Bible verses, and telling us about what she was going through with God and what she was learning."

Natasha was so serious about her faith that she even came up with her own mission statement at ten years old. It was "To love God and purposefully love others." It blew me away to hear this, as many adults haven't taken the time to develop a personal mission statement.

She wrote her parents tributes at age sixteen. She committed herself to a life of purity, steering clear of dating and kissing. She even wanted to give her dad, who had struggled for many years with kidney failure, one of her kidneys. She really was a remarkable young girl who poured out her life into so many others.

In the spring of 2008, Natasha and a group from school went to spend a long weekend at the Outdoor Pursuits Center (OPC). Cool thing about the OPC, it was founded by Sir Edmund Hillary—the first guy to make it to the top of Mt. Everest. Natasha was looking forward to a weekend full of hiking, rock climbing, caving, and ropes courses.

But the weather forecast called for rain. And in New Zealand when it rains, rivers can flood and rise in a hurry. Her mom, Nikki, remembers having to break the bad news about the expected rain to Natasha. Nikki thought for sure Natasha would be disappointed. But Natasha just rolled with it. In fact, she said to her mom, "Oh, Mom, if it rains the whole time, then we'll just jump in the puddles," meaning she was going to make the most of every moment, regardless of the circumstances. That was the kind of person she was. So off they went to the OPC. The rain kept coming. And before long, news reports came in that major flooding had rolled through the OPC, and that some students had been swept away by the floods.

When Andy and Nikki first heard the reports, they knew Natasha would be fine. There were lots of school groups there—she couldn't be one of the ones swept away. But as her mom thought more about it, she became overwhelmed with grief. She said, "I had this overwhelming sadness and I started crying and I said to God, 'Lord, please let Natasha be safe,' and I heard this voice in my spirit say, 'She is safe. She's with me,' and I just remember saying, 'I don't want her with you, I want her with me!'"

They gathered at home with other family and friends, church members, anyone who would come. Later that night there was a knock on the door. When they opened it to a bleary-eyed policeman, everyone immediately knew Natasha was gone.

Her life was over, but her influence was growing. Stories began to come in from friends she had touched. Her mom said, "After the tragedy, people would come up to me saying, 'She put this note in my desk when I was going through a tough time.' She wrote them to her siblings as well." Her dad knew she had been serious about her faith. But after her death, they went into her bedroom closet and found where she had written prayers for teachers, friends, her siblings, and had posted them all over the closet.

Thousands came to the funeral for the seven girls from her school that died, and many latched on to the phrase "jump in puddles," pinning it to their shirts, as a reminder of the life and personality Natasha had. And when her story appeared in the paper, many others latched on to the phrase to find hope and inspiration. The church she attended even adopted her mission statement to keep her story alive.

Her mom said, "When she saw an opportunity to do good, she did it. She invested her life into people. God continues to use her story even today. People are becoming Christians and finding purpose, we keep hearing so many stories."

Natasha wasn't able to give her dad a kidney, but she was able to donate her eyes to someone. Andy said at the funeral, "I know that your eyes will give someone your sight; I just hope they have your vision."[11]

How about you? Do you have a mission statement for your life? Where is your focus? What are you living for? Your identity will ultimately be shaped by your purpose. And living with an eternal focus makes all the difference. It's what really matters.

We've covered the four attributes of a godly woman. That was a ton of information! I've sure learned some things I hope to teach my daughter. And if you come to learn what these four attributes mean—holy beauty, heart of a helper, being a life-giver, and living with an eternal focus—you'll find that living these out will be one of the most exciting experiences of your life. These ought to be the priorities you pursue to become the young woman God created you to be.

6

Between Two Worlds

The Transgender Question

So that's an attempt to outline what the Bible says about the essence of manhood and womanhood. It's a tough thing to do, because just about any trait listed for either gender could be true of the other (like "Engage Others with Wisdom and Grace"—both men *and* women should do that). But I've tried to talk in terms of the *primary* traits for men and women. What patterns appear in Scripture that describe one gender more than the other? What traits describe their role more than the other? Men and women are equally valued before God, but both were created for specific reasons—to accomplish certain things on this earth in a certain way.

But what do you do if you've read these last two chapters and find yourself relating more to the chapter that was supposed to describe the sex that you're not? Or what if deep down inside, you've always really wanted to be the opposite sex than you were born?

You've probably heard about people feeling like they are really a woman trapped in a man's body, or a man inside a woman's body.

Some have asked doctors to help them change into the sex they really feel to be deep inside. People who try to act or dress or live as the sex that is opposite of their biological sex are sometimes referred to as "transgendered." Maybe you've had feelings like this. What should you do?

Start by realizing that there is no perfect man or perfect woman. All men and women fail to properly express their masculinity or femininity at times. Pursuing some ideal of perfect maleness or perfect femaleness is a danger and will leave you facing serious disappointment.

If you don't live up to that image in your head—or even if you do achieve that image—it can still be a disappointment. I've heard it said that the only thing worse than not having goals is achieving them, i.e., sometimes, getting what you want isn't really the best thing. You get there and realize the desire was misguided or shortsighted. I would suspect that a number of people who have attempted to change genders have been surprised by the new challenges they faced.

Just because you find yourself relating more to what our world says is a "boy" thing or a "girl" thing doesn't mean you should have been born with different chromosomes or different levels of testosterone or estrogen, or different genitals. It means that you have a non-traditional path to take to explore your interests.

Not too many years ago, it would have been unthinkable to see two women pair off in the octagon and slug it out for a mixed martial arts (MMA) contest. Not only would it have been unlikely—and in some cases illegal—but they would have been labeled as "manly" or "butch." But now, not only is it becoming popular for women to have a professional MMA career, many of the women are not spoken of in "manly" terms at all. Some are even fashion models on the side. They didn't have to become men to live out their desires of being part of a traditionally manly sport.

Keep in mind that when you're young—and really, for much of life—your desires and feelings and emotions aren't always trustworthy. A common refrain today for reaching happiness in life is to "listen to your heart." But what's far more important is to "lead your heart"—to lead it toward a standard that you can depend on, even if it doesn't completely make sense to you now. And even if it differs with what the culture says is manly or feminine, which is an ever-changing standard.

Take time to ask yourself, "Can I trust that God knows what's best for me?" Or put another way, "Can I trust that He knew that I would have these feelings, and He knew that my body would be the way it is, and yet He allowed me to be created this way?" Can you trust that He can guide you and use you, given the body and mind He's given you?

We have to be careful not to make sex and gender too central to our identity as humans. Yes, your gender and your attractions are deeply important factors in who you become, in shaping your identity. But if they are the *most* defining part of your identity, if who you are rests so squarely on that one thing, then your identity is out of balance.

One writer suggested that changing gender should be a relatively easy thing, saying, "You can choose your gender identity as often as you change your clothes."[1] Is it really that simple? Clothes are an external thing, but something as deeply internal as your gender identity can't possibly be that easy to swap out.

My first car was a 1978 Chevy Malibu. I bought it for eight hundred dollars off a friend at church. It was a great car, but it needed work. The front left fender and part of the front end had been smashed. It was still drivable, but it needed to be repaired. So I called around to the local junkyards and found the parts. I spent half a day with a friend taking the parts off the junked car and getting them home. Then we spent another couple of days installing them and getting everything lined up. The next step was to buff, sand, and prime the new parts to prep them to paint and match the rest of the car. We invested many, many hours of work. At this point, I was ready to move on to another car that already had a sweet paint job, so I never finished the work. But the point was, to make a significant change just to the *appearance* of an eight-hundred-dollar car still took a ton of time and effort, and we didn't even finish the job. How much more would the effort take to change some of the deeper parts of your identity!

Identity goes deeper than what we wear, it goes deeper than what we feel. It's even deeper than our desires, longings, and behaviors. For that reason it's important for a person to tread lightly and think carefully about his or her identity before casting aside some of the things that were given by God.

If you have a friend struggling in this area, listen carefully to them. Ask lots of questions. Reassure them that they can trust you (and make sure you keep their trust!). I heard a man recently recount his approach to counseling a person who wanted to live life as the opposite gender. Before he formed any opinions, he just listened for almost two hours, asking upwards of 150 questions. When's the last time a friend made that kind of time to listen *that* carefully to you about anything? That's an amazing sign of love—to show enough concern to dig that deeply into someone's soul. You'll go a long way toward helping them figure out what to do if you dive in with them and love on them. That doesn't mean you have to approve of all their choices. In fact, real love doesn't ever ignore truth. But real love also doesn't commit senseless acts of truth-ness by just spraying fact statements like a submachine gun at whatever emotion lies in its path. Love applies truth to a teachable heart with care and concern, "according to the need of the moment" (Ephesians 4:29).

Plus, some of these situations are so complex, they take a ton of time to unpack. Your friend might not even know why they are feeling what they feel. How are they supposed to explain it to you? There might be layer upon layer of reasons and emotions involved in the way they live their lives now. Don't be afraid to dive into a complex situation, even when there are no simplistic answers.

When you take a step back from all the noise around this issue today and look at God's design for the world, you see that He established a pretty clear pattern.

He made a man. He made a man who was lonely. And He said that wasn't good. So He made a woman. And His plan was that the two of them—their marriage—would be the basic building block for all of society and civilization. Think about that. God started all of society not with a government, or even a church, but with a family. Of course the man and woman would make mistakes, they wouldn't do things perfectly, but that didn't mean they should toss God's design out the door. And it's no coincidence that so early in the story an enemy started to attack the very essence of this design—and he started by attacking their trust in God. There was a reason God made one of the trees off limits. He really did know what was best for them. But they decided they HAD to have fruit from that tree to be happy. And one of the great and terrible things about God is He will indeed let us pursue the things that we think will give us true happiness. Even if He knows it will hurt us.

This really is the root issue in the entire debate about gender and sexual identity. It's trust in God. Trust in His Word. Trust in His plan and design. You can't put apple juice in your car's gas tank and expect your car to work—even though the apple juice kind of looks like gasoline. And you can't drink gasoline, even though it kind of looks like apple juice. Neither situation will work because the designers of the car, the gas, and the apple juice didn't design things to work that way.

Will you begin to trust that God's design and plan for humanity might actually be the best thing? Will you at least consider it? See if some of the following questions help you process this topic.

- What are some things most often associated with being a man or a woman? [write a few here]

- What are some things you like to do that others might consider more stereotypical of the opposite gender? [list a few out here]

- Now look over that list and try to identify which of those are just a cultural difference, and which are actually core to manhood or womanhood. [mark "cultural" or "core"]

- How do you feel now about these interests in light of these observations?

- Pray and ask God to help you trust that He knew what was best for you when He created you.

SECTION 3

SPIRITUAL IDENTITY

THE MAIN THING

Some kids remember church as drudgery. But I loved it. It was the place to spend time around friends and the adults I admired. I learned so much about life from so many great people. My community was there. Other friends would skip church camp for football or cheerleading camp. Not me. It would have taken an invasion of our hometown by a foreign enemy to keep me away. Summers were back-to-back church activities: church camp, church mission trip, church hiking trip, church Bible studies, church weekend retreats, church leadership training retreats, church softball league, church potlucks and picnics . . . If someone sneezed and it sounded like "ahh-church," I might have shown up with a box of church-issued tissues. Maybe I was weird, or maybe we had a special church (maybe both?), but that's how it was for me.

As much as I loved going to church, and as much as I enjoyed learning new things about the Bible, there came a point after many years of being heavily involved in church where I had to personally come to terms with what it meant to follow Jesus.

Many people experience this later in high school or college, when they begin to question or examine what they were taught growing up. And for many, this results in turning away from the church. In fact, the statistics here are pretty astounding. Forty-three percent of those "who were active church-goers as teenagers . . . will no longer be particularly engaged in a church by their thirtieth birthday."[1]

Why is that? What happened? Was it that they didn't like what their parents believed, found it lacking, just wanted to party without guilt, or something else altogether?

We're going to spend the next couple of chapters really diving into this question. What does it mean to make your faith your own? What does the process look like? How do you navigate it successfully? I hope you'll come away from these chapters with a clear understanding of how you go through this phase, even if you're not there yet.

These really are the most important chapters of this book, and possibly, of your life. Because if you grasp what it means to make your faith your own, you'll have a solid foundation and the tools you'll need to face whatever challenges come your way—both in your teen years and for the rest of your life.

7

Making Your Faith Your Own

Everyone has a set of beliefs that governs their life, whether they realize it or not. Every single decision you make or don't make is shaped by these beliefs. Most people receive a ton of guidance from their parents. But as just noted, 43 percent of teens will ditch what their parents believe after they're out the door. Why is that?

I think there are probably two main things happening.

First, many young Christians have been sold a false message about faith. Many churches today are pushing what has been called moralistic therapeutic deism.[1] Some big words here, but they are important, so let's unpack each one.

Moralistic: Keep the rules and do what you're supposed to do, and God will bless you and life will go the way you want.

Therapeutic: You deserve to have an easy life. God wants you to be happy and for life to go well for you.

Deism: There is a god of some kind out there that is somehow in charge of everything.

This is the message that gets pumped into the brain of students in many churches today—even in Bible-believing churches with leaders who sincerely love Jesus. So you might have grown up hearing this message over and over again, even if it wasn't overt: "There is a God. He wants you to be happy. Keep the rules and He will bless you."

But what happens if something goes wrong? A loved one dies, a big dream doesn't work out, or someone hurts you deeply? Or what if you keep the rules and don't find the promised fulfillment? What happens? Either you keep trying, hoping it will finally work out, or you chuck it out the door like an old summer-league softball T-shirt.

So that's the first thing that many face: Moralistic therapeutic deism just doesn't hold up when real life starts happening.

For some it's a different story. They've grown up hearing another message. For as long as they can remember, they've heard that sin is bad. That doing worldly things is unfulfilling and will send you to hell. They heard a legalistic message that made some activities (like dancing, playing cards, listening to "secular" music, watching movies, or going to Disney World) sound like the very devil himself came up with the ideas. So when they tried some of these off-limits activities and found they were actually kind of fun, they felt they'd been lied to. And that killed the credibility of what they were taught growing up.

I have no idea where you fall in this spectrum. Were you fed a shallow faith or forced to flee from fun-land—or some combination of the two? Or neither? Maybe you had a perfect church? Only you can speak to that. But here's what I do know. You have to figure out what you're going to do with Jesus in light of what you've been given. No one else can do this for you. Sure, many others will be *part* of that journey, but ultimately you have to come to terms with who Jesus *was*, and who He *is* today. Will He be the central part of your life? Or will He just be another name you studied in history class and then forgot about like Genghis Khan or Alexander the Great? They were both important people, but they probably have no bearing on the way you live your daily life.

For me, there came a point where I realized there were billions of people on this earth who had either never heard the name *Jesus*, or had chosen to follow a different faith. *Billions*. That was hard to believe. So did that mean they were all wrong? Or did that mean that I was wrong? What did it mean? Could BILLIONS of people be wrong? And have I just been following my parents' ideas because that's what they believe? It's frightening to think you might have been secretly tricked into becoming like your parents. Yikes! Conspiracy theory for sure.

Be encouraged. When you get to this place, it's actually a really good thing. It might be scary or confusing, but it means you're dealing with the real issue. You're not just going through the motions anymore. You're not just following a religion but moving toward a real relationship. You're actually learning to walk on your own. You're starting the process of making your faith your own.

Why Faith?

Before we talk about how to make your faith your own, we have to ask why. Why faith? Why not just live as life comes to you? Why do you need a "faith system," or set of beliefs to follow? Some would say it's rather silly to follow a religion based on some ancient document written to people who probably didn't own a pair of underwear, a toothbrush, or even know how to write their own name. No way they could have figured out how to send a text message on their own. How in the world can that relate to us today?

Well, let's talk about humanity. You've probably noticed there are some differences between humans and animals. Besides excessive body hair (I'm talking about the animals), there's one thing in particular that really sets us apart. Consider that no lion ever wakes on the Serengeti and finds itself wrestling with a lingering inner turmoil over the question of their purpose on that plain.

They don't ponder deep thoughts like, *Why am I here? What was I made for? Why am I so violent toward cute little gazelle fawns? Why do I just want to rip them apart?* There are no wildlife therapy office stops on safari tours.

But almost every human ever born wonders about the meaning of life, the reason for their existence, if their life will make a difference or not, will they be remembered after they're gone? They question their behaviors, even ones they feel compelled to do. The way you think about these issues and the way you go about answering the big questions in life and finding purpose and meaning will determine the way you live. And there are some big differences between the ways people have gone about this. Mother Teresa found her answers in serving others. Hitler eliminated others.

You see, everyone has some sort of governing authority for life, a set of principles they follow to make decisions. It might be something they read at church, or it might be their favorite celebrity social media feed. It might be emotions. They might be trying to model their life after a favorite TV character. Whatever it is, *something* serves as a final authority in the life of every single person, even if they don't really realize it.

So here's the question you have to wrestle with: What is your governing authority? What serves as your moral compass? How do you make decisions in life? And how do you know when you've made the right ones or the wrong ones? What's it based on?

Take a second to look over the list on the next page and check any and all that apply for you.

The reality is there are so many voices shouting at you in an attempt to control your life. Some shout louder than others. Some of that shouting is easy to block out. Some you are drawn to like a toddler to a snow-cone stand. Some you want to follow even when you feel like you shouldn't.

It's kind of a trick question, though, because there might not be just one thing that governs the way you live. You might make decisions based on some wacky combination of all of the above.

I figure out right from wrong in life primarily based on:
- [ ] reason
- [ ] history
- [ ] emotions
- [ ] logic
- [ ] approval of friends
- [ ] whatever my parents say
- [ ] feelings
- [ ] what I learn at school
- [ ] church
- [ ] Bible
- [ ] books/stories
- [ ] movies/TV
- [ ] experiences in life
- [ ] other family members

You might not even know what it is. That doesn't mean you're weird. I think most people, if really pressed to answer this question, would struggle to identify their ultimate authority in life.

Nonetheless, it's still important. In fact, it's the most important question you'll face. Ever. Because it determines how you live and how you try to find meaning and purpose in life.

Authority

Ultimately, the only way you can have any kind of dependable authority is to find something utterly dependable (welcome to the department of redundancy department). Friends, movies, parents, actors, reason, emotions, and yes, even yourself, they'll all let you down. They'll never be able to perfectly guide you through life. You have to have a perfect standard you can depend on perfectly. Something that will bear up under the weight of life.

One of my favorite writers, an influential Christian thinker in the 1960s and '70s, Francis Schaeffer, had this to say about the importance of choosing a belief system that will hold up under whatever pressures you try to load on top of it:

> The Romans built little humpbacked bridges over many of the streams of Europe. People and wagons went over these safely for centuries. But if people today drove heavily loaded trucks over these bridges, they would break. It is this way with the lives and value systems of individuals and cultures when they have nothing stronger to build on than their own limitedness, their own finiteness. They can stand when pressures are not too great, but when pressures mount, if then they do not have a sufficient base, they crash—just as a Roman bridge would cave in under the weight of a modern . . . truck.[2]

So where can you find an authority that dependable? Where in the world does that even exist? We live in a world of so much fakeness—so much pretends to be real, like banana *flavoring* (is it really that hard to use actual bananas? I mean, come on! They're the most abundant fruit on earth!). So much appears to be real when it is not. And just when you need it the most, it falls apart. How can you find something that you can absolutely base your life on in this crazy world?

The Power of the Word of God

The one thing that will stand all tests for authenticity, credibility, reliability, and applicability is the Word of God—the Bible.

Some might say, "The Bible? Really? Didn't people use that to justify all kinds of atrocities in history?" For sure that has happened. But just because something is used toward an evil end doesn't mean the thing itself is evil. I can make the Bible say whatever I want by ripping certain verses out of context. But that's not really fair to the Bible. And to be completely honest about history, twentieth-century atheism resulted in some pretty horrific atrocities as well—with millions of people killed in wars across the globe. So just chucking the Bible isn't going to solve the problem. Because what you end up with might be worse. You have to approach it fairly and try to figure out what it's really about before you write it off.

Here's what makes the Bible so incredibly powerful: Hebrews 4:12 says, "The word of God is living and active and sharper than any two-edged sword." It's not just an ancient document written to an ancient people—it's alive—it engages with the heart and mind and "pierces to the division of soul and spirit, joint and marrow, discerning the thoughts and intentions of the heart." God's Word is the ultimate source of authority for life. And not just because it has good ideas. Not just because it is utterly dependable and reliable. But because in it we find God himself. We get to know Him through its pages and come to love Him and follow Him.

You see, being a follower of Christ is not just about going to a church—it's about a whole life commitment. And when you commit your life to Christ—a person, not just a system—you have committed yourself to the very Creator of the universe. Who better to trust with your life than the One who designed life? He will never let you down. He will always be there for you: "I will never leave you nor forsake you" (Hebrews 13:5 ESV).

The Power of Surrender

Imagine living in the realm of King Arthur. There was a point where knights or maidens placed themselves under the rule of the king, kneeling before him, offering themselves in a completely vulnerable state, and as the king lowered the sword to their shoulder, he welcomed them in. By their prostrate position before him they were saying, "I commit myself wholeheartedly to the purposes of your kingdom. I give my life in service to you." That's a big step, and it's a noble step. It doesn't mean that they are instantly equipped to accomplish everything the king has for them, but it does mean their allegiances have changed.

There needs to be a point where you take the step to place yourself under the rule and reign of someone greater than yourself. You no longer live on your own. You no longer live for self, but you join a kingdom and become a member of a royal family.

How Do You Surrender?

So how do you come to submit yourself to Jesus? How do you turn your life over to Him, and live in His kingdom, under His rule and reign?

It starts by admitting and accepting a few truths about the state you are in right now.

You did nothing to have life as good as you do. Back in the first chapter, we addressed the crazy idea of the "self-made man" or "self-made woman." Remember all those things you had absolutely nothing to do with? Your parents, skin color, brain power, birth place, birth time, culture, society, accessible health care, education, on and on . . . What did you do to earn those things? Nothing. Not a thing. The sooner you can realize this, the more you can live your life full of gratitude for all that you benefit from every single day (like paved roads, running water, sewer systems, electrical grids, and cell towers). God was gracious to allow you to be born the way you were in the time you were. Even if your life isn't perfect and you've had major challenges, you still have much you can be grateful for that you did nothing to earn. You've got it pretty good, and you didn't go get it yourself.

We have all actively rebelled against God's goodness throughout our entire lives. This is true of every person ever born. Romans 3:23 says, "For all have sinned and fall short of the glory of God." Every single one of us has given God the middle finger. That's a harsh way to put it, but it's true. In a sense we've said to Him, "No, thanks. I don't want you to rule over my life. I want to do things my way when I want to do it and how I want to do it." We're all like a toddler sprinting toward a street full of traffic just to be free from the parent trying to control him. That kind of freedom has a cost, though.

You are in desperate need of being rescued from this situation. Yes, you've rebelled against God, and you're headed toward an awful end, even if you don't realize it. It may not feel that way now, but there's no more dangerous place to be than living life apart from God. You've pushed off from the bank of His protective hand and are floating along pleasantly on the raft of your own preferences. Yet Niagara Falls looms around the bend. Romans 6:23 says, "The wages of sin is death." The wages, or the payment, you receive for rejecting God is the very thing you wanted—separation from Him, which is death. Death began with Adam and Eve at the very beginning of the Bible and it continues on today. It happens to everyone physically, and some choose to endure spiritual death as well.

You can't get out of this situation on your own. When you're floating down the middle of a river, with no oar, no motor, and not enough time to swim to shore, there's nothing you can do to be rescued. You need someone to stretch a cable across the river so that you can latch on and be pulled out before plummeting over the falls. Romans 6:23 continues, ". . . but the free gift of God is eternal life in Christ Jesus our Lord." You don't even have to drop a token in a machine to have a lifeline thrown your way. The gift of life is completely free.

And here's the amazing part. Not only is it free—it is *freeing*. It frees you from slavery to self, from worry, from self-reliance, from egotism, from a sense of purposelessness, from pursuing the wrong sense of purpose. It frees you from finding success in the wrong things. Jesus offers, in Matthew 11:28–29, "Come to Me, all who are weary and heavy-laden, and I will give you rest. Take My yoke upon you and learn from me, for I am gentle and humble in heart, and you will find rest for your souls."

Why Jesus? What's special about Him? The good news of His life is that He lived a perfect life. And yet wicked men still executed Him out of jealousy and bitterness. They thought killing Him would end the problems He caused undermining their religious schemes. But He didn't stay dead. In fact, He is the only person to die and bring himself back to life. He conquered the power that death has on humanity and paved a way for us to find true life in Him.

All you have to do is ask. Just ask. There really is nothing else you can do. You can't do enough to gain His favor. That's like digging out of a hole you're stuck in. It won't work. No, you need someone to wander by with a rope, and you need to ask them for help. You need to submit yourself to His rule and reign in your life.

Many people find prayer to be one of the best ways to take this step. But to be clear, a prayer isn't some magic chant that unlocks a wardrobe-door portal into a new world. It's more about putting words to what is already happening inside of you. A prayer might look something like this: "God, you are so amazing. You made me and this world, and you gave me so much that I've taken for granted. I'm sorry for that. Thank you. Thank you so much. I'm sorry I've run from you. I've wanted to do things my own way. I didn't want to follow you, even though you know what's best for me. Please help me to follow you. Please forgive me for my sins—for rejecting you and running toward things that are sorry substitutes for the real thing. I commit my life now to following you. I know I won't be perfect, but I want to live my life for you now instead of for myself or for whatever it was that seemed so important before. Thank you for sending Jesus to die for me. Thank you for bringing Him back to life to live for me. Please help me to follow you in all that I do."

Maybe you aren't in a place where you're ready to make a commitment like this. I get that—and I respect that. I've been there too. But here's what I'd encourage you to do: List out your questions and seek out answers. Write out your big questions and go find people who can help answer them. I promise there are really good answers out there to your unanswered questions.

A Sense of Urgency

Nabeel Qureshi, who grew up as a Muslim, became good friends with a Christian in high school. And they began debating at great length the differences between Islam and Christianity. There came a point where Nabeel didn't really want to keep talking about it, but his friend pushed him to keep pressing into his questions, and so Nabeel continued. For years they dialogued, till Nabeel finally came to see that much of what he believed did not really have a basis for belief like he thought. At that point he had some huge choices to make: follow Islam out of tradition, live in intentional ignorance, or turn to Christ, the One in whom he had found the answers to his real questions. That's a hard place to be, but it's a good place to be.[3]

You really need to have some sense of urgency about this. There's no need to put it off. The reality is, you're not guaranteed another single day of life.

A few years ago a tornado hit the area near where I live. It was a huge one, estimated to be a half-mile wide at one point. It devastated hundreds of homes, ripped up all kinds of trees and buildings. If you've never seen a tornado or aren't familiar with their insanely destructive power, imagine dozens of bulldozers rumbling through your neighborhood operating jet-engine-powered pressure washers. It creates a gigantic mess and leaves a wide path of destruction.

It's been years since that event, yet when you drive through those neighborhoods you can still see the bare spots left behind from the trees that were ripped up. And the trees still standing look like a field of splintered Popsicle sticks left over from a failed third-grade science fair project.

I've got a good friend whose home was hit by this tornado. It pretty much decimated his house in about thirty seconds. In the aftermath photos, it looks like a couple of those elephants from my neighborhood just leaned up against the second floor of his house, pushed it over, then dragged it over to the pond for a bath. Not the best way to care for your second floor.

Just before the tornado hit, there was a moment when he was moving his family into their safe-room closet (they have those in Tornado Land). He knew this tornado was going to hit their house, so he said to his family, "This is real. This could be your last moment on earth. If you've never committed your life to Christ, then now is the time, no more waiting." Of course, that's a pretty intense situation—and as you would expect, his family was taking that prayer pretty seriously. But even though there's no tornado in your front yard, you need to have that same sense of urgency about your life now. You're not guaranteed another day.

That same tornado hit the house of another family I know; in fact, I had seen the dad at the office a few days before. Their house was completely leveled. It looks like it never even existed. The mom and seven of the kids lived through it, but sadly, the dad and two daughters didn't survive.

It was urgent for the first family, but it was essential for the second. They didn't get another chance.

I remember kneeling and sincerely praying for Christ to come into my life at five years old, yet as I wrote earlier, it wasn't until my teen years that I wrestled with making my faith my own. I could no longer avoid the hard questions. And it wasn't always pretty. I ignored some questions for a while and wrestled with God for a while. But at the end of the day, it became obvious that there was nowhere else to find real life. Nothing else could bear up under the weight of testing. Jesus was the only one who could be fully depended on in every situation, in every moment. And so I committed anew to follow Him. And it hasn't been perfect. I've still sinned. I've still been stubborn and self-centered and arrogant and . . . wait, I think that's enough of my sin for now. The point is, life isn't perfect, even if you have Christ as your Lord and guide, but it is new now. It is built on a foundation that will last, and it is through Him that you will experience real life to its fullest.

Growing in Your Walk with God

here's a time in life when you want to be an adult in some ways but want to stay a kid in other ways. I remember when playing with Transformers was still kind of fun, yet at the same time I wanted a job at a local grocery store. Life is all about transitions. We go from one major phase to another. You have to figure out how to navigate through transitions, or you'll get left behind, stuck in between two different phases, like a boy in a circus sideshow covered in man-size body hair. Gross.

Once you commit to following Christ and have given your life to Him, you've begun the most amazing journey you'll experience. But don't stay stuck as an infant— a baby Christian. Start growing so that you don't have to be led around by the hand. Figure out how to walk on your own.

Growing as a Christian is like growing in other things—it takes time, learning, and developing some practices and habits. It's not always easy, but it's also not rocket science. There are a few things that if you learn to do well and do regularly, will help you grow rapidly.

Spiritual Disciplines

The practices that many Christians follow to grow closer to God are often referred to as spiritual disciplines.

Just like if you want to get better at sports, music, cooking, or art, you need to develop some skills and practice them. Run some sprints, lift some weights, practice scales and progressions, study recipes, and draw, draw, draw. Eventually you develop a level of competency that you can build upon. You get better through practice.

Now, I don't know that I like saying you can "get better at being a Christian." That sounds weird. The goal here is not "getting better" but rather, getting closer to God. And these disciplines, or practices, if done with a humble heart that truly seeks God, will draw you closer to Him. We can trust this is true because they show up in the Bible and we're encouraged to do them.

Where to Start

There are many different practices we could follow—and I'd encourage you to grab a book on spiritual disciplines and read through it to learn more than we can cover here.[1] But there are three big ones to get you started: Bible study, prayer, and community.

Bible Study

Don Whitney, an expert on the spiritual disciplines, says, "If you are not growing in the Word of God, it is hard to imagine a person growing, at least over any length of time. Because this is the standard [of] Christlikeness revealed to us, and . . . the food for the soul that helps us grow."[2] The Word of God, the Bible, is like food for your spiritual growth. You have to be consuming it to grow.

So how do you do this?

Well, pretty simply, start by reading it. Some swear that reading at least a chapter a day is best. That way it becomes a habit, and it takes only five minutes. I love Scripture Union's top one hundred Bible passages.[3] They've structured a reading schedule program so that if you read the one hundred passages, each about a chapter in length, and you can check off the boxes as you go, you'll have a good overview of the major stories and teachings of the Bible. Even though it's a bite-size amount, each day you'll keep growing and growing, little by little. Before too long you will have read tons of Scripture. That's kind of the middle-of-the-road approach.

If you like to do things all out, you might try reading through the entire Bible in a year. That's a little over three chapters a day and takes probably fifteen or twenty minutes. Or choose one of the many great Bible reading plans out there. Some take you straight through the Bible. One of my favorites is by The Navigators and has daily readings from the Old Testament and the New.[4] Or you can buy a one-year Bible and it will tell you what to read based on what day of the year it is.

If you are the minimalist type, you can drop way down to a verse a day. Let me tell you, this approach can be powerful. One year I spent about ten weeks going through part of the Sermon on the Mount (Matthew chapters five through seven) with a group of guys. Some days I would read only a couple of verses. It's a powerful way to dwell on the meaning and application of these verses. The Sermon on the Mount is so rich, it's wise to go slowly to get the most out of it.[5]

It's good to employ all three approaches by mixing it up. Some years I've crazily tried to read through the Bible twice (never made it). Other years I've gone minimalist, and others somewhere in between. It all depends on what season of life you're in. If you're a new Christian, I think it's pretty powerful to read through the Bible in a year. There's no better way to get your mind around all that is in there. You'll be amazed by how doing this even once will change the way you read the Bible. It's valuable even if you don't understand every word. (Tip: If you get bogged down in a really detailed part, like Leviticus, read fast through those parts.) The first time I read through the entire Bible, it was so incredible to see how all the stories I heard as a kid were connected. I had no idea they related like that.

Whatever way you go about it, the important thing is to actually do it—to read the Bible regularly.

I remember hearing one of my favorite Bible teachers, Tommy Nelson, talk about a commitment he made to never let a day go by without studying the Bible. At that time he said he had pretty much kept that commitment, other than the day his son was born. . . . (But he reviewed some Scripture he had memorized that day, so I think that counts.) I found that pretty inspiring. I wanted to have that kind of commitment to growing in God's Word—yet it can be pretty intimidating; that's a serious commitment to make!

You may think, *No way I could find time to read a chapter a day.* But you will always find time to do what's important to you. You always do. Don't believe me? When I worked with college students, I remember some were really growing and diligently studying God's Word, while others would repeatedly lament that they just couldn't find the time. I used to buy that line—until I realized that those same students had no problem finding several hours during finals week to watch movies. What they meant was, "It's not important enough to find the time." The crazy part is, college is when you'll have the most discretionary time *ever* in your life. If you can't learn to make it a priority then, you probably will struggle to do so later.

So do what you can to find the time. I know guys who swear by their Bible app. It tells them what to read every day. It will even read the Bible to them in the car. Sweet.

It's important to read the Bible, but here's the really important thing to understand about Bible study: It's no magic formula. You don't turn into Saint Awesome just by reading thirty-seven verses a day. First Corinthians 8:1 says, "Knowledge puffs up, but love builds up" (ESV). I've known some folks who were pretty serious Bible students but weren't always the nicest to be around. There are plenty of people with knowledge of the Bible whose hearts haven't been transformed. The best example of this is Satan himself. He even quoted Scripture to Jesus, trying to use the Bible to tempt Him! That's scary. So don't turn Bible study into an idol. The Bible is meant to point us to Christ and to help us grow to become more like Him. It's meant to transform and renew your mind, just like Romans 12:2 says.

Here are other tools to help you drill God's Word into your head.

MEDITATION

Meditation is not some form of mystical chanting. It's dwelling intently on truth until it gets deep in your head. Don Whitney says, "Reading is the exposure to Scripture, but meditation is the absorption of Scripture."[6] You have to intentionally engage with what you're reading to take it from information to something that is life-changing.

JOURNALING

Journaling can be one of the best forms of meditation. It slows you down and gives you time needed to think about the meaning of the verses you've read. I've been journaling for over twenty years now; it really is fun to go back and read journal entries and see how God has worked in my life. It's easy to forget the slow change that happens over time, but journaling helps you to remember. Some people journal right in their Bibles, marking and coloring all along the way to help ideas stick. That can be loads of fun, especially if you have an artistic side.

SCRIPTURE MEMORIZATION

Probably the most powerful way to meditate on Scripture is to memorize it. There are tons of ways to go about this, but the simplest method is to simply repeat it. Apps can help—but having friends join you helps even more. Seeds Family Worship has Scripture memory songs that help as well. Start by memorizing Psalm 119:9–11.

So that's our first big spiritual discipline: Bible study. Now for the other two.

Prayer

If Bible Study is how *God* communicates to *us*, then prayer is how *we* communicate to *God*. At its most basic level, prayer is simply talking with God.

But prayer, though simple, can be surprisingly hard work. You might kneel with a determined resolve to stay in a penitent posture until you've prayed for every friend in your class. Perhaps you've carved out thirty minutes—enough time to go deep—so you start and go at it with gusto. Then after what seems like a solid seven days, praying for every student, parent, sibling, and pet you know of at school, you look up at the clock to see exactly three minutes and forty-nine seconds has passed. What? How can that be?

Here's one of the challenges with prayer. Many people, when they pray, only come to God to ask Him to do things for them or others. That's 90 percent of their prayer life. But imagine if you approached other relationships that way. Or reverse it: Imagine if you had a friend who only came to you to ask for things. If every conversation with them started with, "Will you please give me _____?" How long would you want to be around that pal? After about the third time, you'd learn to dart the opposite direction when they entered the room.

God's not going to run off and hide in a janitor closet from you. But if you want to get to know Him better, start praying more like the way you talk with anyone else you want to get to know. You tell them about your day, you wonder what they like, you tell them thanks for things, you ask them questions about life for understanding. You tell them what you like about them. You drop compliments when they do something well. And sometimes you just enjoy hanging out with them; no agenda, and maybe very little talking.

Prayer is like that. There are times when you'll have a long and deep conversation with God, just like with a close friend. But there are plenty of other times when you'll drop in quickly. I don't think you can text God yet, but it's kind of like that. And then there are other times still where you sit quietly without much talking at all.

Any growing relationship has different types of communication, and every relationship goes through seasons. Prayer is like that. It can also help to have some guidelines for prayer—some lists to pray through or some categories to pray about. Donald Whitney recommends praying through the Psalms, meaning, reading through a psalm and praying parts of it back to God as you go.[7] I like praying through Deuteronomy 6:4–9, and the Lord's Prayer, Matthew 6:9–13.

But you can't turn prayer into a formula any more than you can turn a friendship into a formula. Though there sure have been people who tried.

In the mid 1500s, one of the most powerful men in the world, the king of Spain, Philip II (for whom the Philippines were named), had a son dying of an illness. So the king swore a pact with God, saying, "If you'll do a miracle for me and heal my son, I'll do a miracle for you." When God healed his son, he paid God back by having a prayer robot made. You can still see it operate in the Smithsonian. It's a Robo-monk, a prayer-bot, that when wound up goes through a series of motions imitating the standard prayer practices of the day. The thinking was that this little robot could offer up much more prayer and do it more perfectly, thus bringing more honor to God than any person ever could.[8]

Prayer is not like that. God isn't looking for us to turn into prayer machines. That would be pretty creepy for sure. No, He wants to get to know us, and for us to get to know Him. He wants us to talk to Him like a friend, but also like a respected mentor. Getting to know Him through prayer is one of the most exciting parts of the Christian life. And watching Him work in your life and the life of others through prayer will blow your mind.

I remember when I had a very strong disdain for openly homosexual persons. But the more I read about Jesus, the more I realized He would have been hanging out with them and loving them. So I began to pray for opportunities to befriend those living that lifestyle, to get to know them. Before long I landed a job that happened to have me working closely with a handful of homosexual men. And it turned out to be an amazing experience. Because once I knew those guys, I no longer had to villainize them. They were *people* struggling with life, just like I was. They expressed it differently, and they may not have had Christ to help them with that struggle, but I no longer had to disdain or fear them. I had some great conversations with a few of them about Christ. I didn't preach, but as we became friends, and they saw the peace I experienced, they wanted to know more. It was definitely an answer to prayer.

You can come to Christ in prayer—you can bring anything to Him—your hurts, your needs, your insecurities, your desires, whatever it might be. He wants to hear from you. And watching Him work through prayer is one of the most amazing experiences you will have in this life.

Community

You desperately need relationships with other Christians to grow as a Christian. The second greatest commandment requires you to "love your neighbor as yourself" (Mark 12:31). Isolating yourself isn't an option. In fact, when any friend of mine starts to pull away and get isolated, it's always a sign that something is wrong. Proverbs 18:1 says, "Whoever isolates himself seeks his own desire; he breaks out against [or rejects] all sound judgment" (ESV). When you get isolated you lose perspective. You make too big a deal out of little things or minimize big things. I've seen guys justify all kinds of wrongs when they are isolated. One guy who had been a spiritual mentor of mine justified a divorce based on some wacky interpretations of Scripture. He ended up there partly because he was isolated. Growing as a Christian requires that you be in community with other Christians.

Hebrews 10:25 (ESV) says you should not "neglect meeting together." I know some will say, "Going to church doesn't make you a Christian any more than going to Chick-fil-A makes you a cow." True, but the Bible doesn't command you to go to Chick-fil-A (though I'm sure some have searched hard for that verse). And though church is great, going to church isn't the only time you should be in community. It's one place for that to happen, but if it's the only place community happens, you won't be experiencing the depth of community that Christ has in mind for you.

You also can't really live out many of the basic commands of Scripture, what some have called the "one-anothers" if you're not in community. So it's a pretty important thing.

So these are three of the big spiritual disciplines, but there are several others like evangelism, giving, and serving others. Make sure you're taking time to learn about those practices as well.

Hungry? Thirsty?

Now, what do you do if you find yourself with little desire to read the Bible, pray, or spend time worshiping with other Christians?

I had a friend who quit reading the Bible altogether because she just wasn't "feeling it." She said, "You know, it seems that it's not going to do much good to read the Bible if your heart's not in the right place."

But the exact opposite is true! There really is no more important time to read the Bible than if your heart is distant from God. What better way to get back to Him than to hear from Him! Sometimes you have to feel your way into action, but often you need to act your way into feeling.

Maybe Bible study has become a bit boring for you. That doesn't mean you should give it up any more than you would give up eating, drinking, or breathing just because you're bored. Maybe you need to make some changes to the *way* you're approaching the Bible. Don't give up on what might possibly be the most important part of your life—connecting with God. If your heart isn't in it, try to dig in deep and ask why.

I used to play a fair amount of guitar. I was fine playing worship songs, even playing in front of the church. But I wanted to get better.

I wanted to learn some solos and riffs to expand my skills. I worked at it for a while, but I became frustrated by the lack of progress. Around that time a friend surprised me with a pair of tickets for a Phil Keaggy concert. Phil is widely considered one of the greatest guitar players ever, which is especially amazing given that he's missing a finger on his right hand. So watching him move up and down the neck of his guitar at that concert was mesmerizing and inspiring. I went home and began my venture anew. And though I never came anywhere near his level, I kept improving. And so the phrase that stuck with me coming out of that experience was, "When you're in a rut, go see live music."

When you're in a rut spiritually, find a way to get some inspiration. Could be a book, could be a conversation with someone you respect, or maybe a conference or a video online. Or maybe serve in a homeless shelter. But here's the deal: Don't give in to your apathy. If you were to do that with eating, drinking, or breathing, you'd die. Instead, keep fighting for your spiritual life, don't give up, find a way to connect with God and work through the apathy.

Another Reason Why This Is Important

We've been talking about the importance of making your faith your own. You have to know what you believe and why you believe it. And whatever you believe, the moral code upon which you base your life has to be strong enough to bear up under the challenges you encounter. Otherwise it will crumble when you need it most.

But there's another reason why building your faith on something that will last is important, and it's not just about you. It's about the future. It's about all that will follow. What will you pass on to the next generations? Your life is laying a foundation. Is it something others can build on as well? Or are you passing on a foundation that doesn't provide much support?

Francis Schaeffer's writings have had a huge influence on my life, so much so that my wife and I named one of our children after him. The story of his ministry to students in Europe after World War II was incredibly inspiring.[9] One of the things Schaeffer noticed happening with the American church troubled him; this quote sums it all up:

> The generation of those who first give up on biblical inerrancy may have a warm evangelical background and real personal relationship with Jesus Christ so that they can "live theologically" on the basis of their "limited inerrancy" viewpoint. But what happens when the next generation tries to build on that?[10]

Okay, I know that's a loaded quote, so let's unpack it. He's saying that those who give up on the trustworthiness of the Bible (i.e., biblical inerrancy) might be able to keep going along just fine in their Christian life. It might not affect them too much at all. But what about those who come afterwards? Can you pass along a view of the Bible that is wishy-washy? Very few people get excited about that. If you teach the Bible but begin by saying, "You know, some of this is great, some is hogwash, some I don't know what to do with, and we don't really know if any of it is true, but you should listen carefully and try to model your life after it," any group of somewhat intelligent human beings will check out in a hurry.

So make your faith your own, and base that faith on the authority of God's timeless, completely trustworthy holy Word. That is a foundation you can build your life on AND pass on to the next generation. Because life isn't about you. It isn't about me either. If we can get that in our heads, the world will be a better place, and we'll both be happier.

RELATIONAL IDENTITY

THE PEOPLE WHO SHAPE YOU

U p to this point in life, your parents have probably had more influence on you than any other relationships. Remember back to the first chapter, where we talked about all the well-being stats? Yeah, your parents really have shaped you in a BIG way. But now you're probably starting to look to your friends more for approval, for ideas about how to live and how to spend your time, and to help determine what's important to you. In fact, you probably spend more time with your friends than your parents. And that's okay. That's part of growing up.

You're also looking to people older than you for ideas. Your teachers, coaches, even your parents' friends—they all have a ton to offer. You're also probably a whole lot more interested in a special someone than you used to be. Ever find yourself walking out of the way just so you can see that guy or girl before class? Even for just a glimpse? All these relationships play a big role in who you are becoming.

There's a quote that has caused me to think more about the importance of relationships. It says, "You are the average of the five people you spend the most time with."[1] Wow. Really? It may not be an exact formula, but the point is that the people you spend the most time around will influence you—whether positively or negatively—so you should fight like mad to do whatever it takes to get around the people you want to be like.

This is especially important for a few groups of people: friends, mentors, and your romantic interests. How do you navigate these relationships in this season of life? Sometimes it's great and easy, but sometimes there are huge struggles and loads of awkwardness. But if that above quote is true, then you need to think carefully about who you spend your time with.

So you have a choice. Will you hang out with whoever, whenever, and let your life be shaped by them? Or will you be intentional to surround yourself with people you know will make you better? The choice is yours. Maybe you can't hang out with everyone you prefer, but you also don't have to let yourself be dragged down by someone who drains the life out of you.

So how can you be intentional with your relationships? Well, let's talk about each of these three groups.

Friends

here's a group of guys I know that when they were your age, they started meeting together for a Bible study. Their dads started the group because they wanted to help their sons learn about manhood. But after the study ended, the young men kept meeting without their dads, and before long, they made accountability a central focus of the group. They began to pray for one another, to support one another, to call each other up to godly living. They called themselves the Roof Crashers after the guys in Mark 2:4–5, who ripped a hole in the roof of a house so they could lower their sick bro down to Jesus. Now that's dedication. I mean, think about this for a minute. Imagine you and three close friends grab your partly paralyzed pal, drag her up on top of the house next door, rip a hole in the roof, and finally, somehow lower her down to the kitchen floor without dropping her on her head. That's some serious effort! Not to mention that most of my neighbors don't get all giddy about people peeling back their shingles.

That kind of friendship doesn't just happen. *Maybe* three random people would do that for you, but more than likely it would be someone you were already tight with. But it is really hard to make those kinds of friends. You might have tons of people you call "friend," but what about finding a *true* friend—someone who will be there for you no matter what? That doesn't just happen. You have to go through some stuff together. You have to have some good times but also some hard times, and stick with it even when you might want to give up on the friendship.

I still remember meeting my very first friend. It was inside the pale block walls of our first-grade Sunday school class. The room smelled like fresh paint, Lysol, and fruit punch. I was in a three-piece suit and tie (that's how five-year-olds rolled in my 'hood). The class was seated in a circle in those toddler-sized blue plastic chairs, and he walked over and said, "Hi." That started a twenty-year friendship—until we went our separate ways after college. I moved out of town, and we didn't keep up. He was my closest friend in life up until then; he was a true friend. He was always there for me; he accepted me as I was but still challenged me; and he never, ever, *ever* put me down. We shared tons of laughs, but some hard times too. And now he's gone. A few weeks ago he passed away. And now I regret that I didn't do a better job of staying in touch. I missed a lot of amazing moments, but also some hard moments, and I wasn't there for him when he was struggling. Why the regret? Because how many true friends do you really have in this life? How many friends can you say accept you unconditionally? It's rare. You are lucky if you end up with one or two friends like that.

If you find a true friend like that, you better do all you can to keep him or her, especially as you grow older, because they get harder to find. In fact, I'm realizing now that there is almost no greater use of time than building into your friendships, because life was meant to be lived in relationship. How do we know this? Look at Jesus' life.

It would seem that the one person on earth who wouldn't need friends would be Jesus. God in human form. He could get along without pals, right? But what did He do? He found twelve dudes and hung out with them everywhere, almost all the time. He was constantly pouring His life into them. He even called them friends. They didn't always understand Him, and sometimes they argued about which one Jesus liked best, but they were there. He had a closer circle with three of them, and one that was the closest. If friends were important to Jesus, then they should be to us.

But here's the hard part: Making friends can look really different for guys versus girls. Both need friendships, but guys and girls don't make friends the same way.

Guys and Friends

I remember in high school there was this one guy who always annoyed me. Always. Especially when we played basketball. Finally one day we had it out. We really went at it, mostly just yelling and shoving and posturing like we might throw a real punch. Not long after that, we became close friends. We even started meeting in the mornings to memorize the entire book of Philippians. No lie!

Ask a few guys you know and I bet they've had that happen. After a big fight they become the best of friends. Or you show up to a party, see someone wearing your same shirt, and you're like, "HHHHEEEYYYY!!!! COOL SHIRT!!!!!!" and you become best friends.

You may have heard of the TV series *Band of Brothers*, based on the story of a group of guys in World War II. The military has done research to try to figure out what makes guys bond so tightly during really intense times like wartime. Is it because they are out fighting for "the cause," or for their country, or for a leader they admire? Those are all important reasons, but the main reason they fight and work together was for the guys in their unit; for the survival of the buddies next to them on the battle line.

One author described that kind of bond with one word: love. There's no better expression of love than to lay down your life for someone else, and that's what soldiers do for one another.[1]

The other crazy thing researchers discovered was that the closer guys are on the battlefield—and off—the less stressed they are. Their strong friendships make everything easier. Jumping out of airplanes, gearing up for battle—all of the really intense situations experienced in war—everyone is calmer when they know the guys next to them care and have their back.

So dudes can bond quickly even in crazy tense situations.

Girls and Friendships

For girls, things seem to be a little different. Some of the same things are true for girls as they are for boys—like how friends make life better and easier and less stressful—but girls seem to have a harder time getting close. Teenage girls seem more like porcupines at times. Everything's fine until you get too close, and then your face turns into a pincushion for knitting needles. Ouch.

There's even a label for this: mean girls.

My neighbor said his daughter had a friend turn mean on her. The first couple of years in school, they were best friends. But then his daughter made the homecoming court, and her friend didn't. And his daughter won student of the year, and her friend didn't. And all of a sudden her former best friend became the enemy. She went ugly on her and rallied other girls to help tear down the school star. It was so bad that my neighbor's daughter told her parents, "I don't want another award. It's not worth it" (a sentence few boys have ever uttered).

Social media can make things even harder. When I was a kid (back in prehistoric times, before the internet or mobile phones), if someone was going to be mean, they mostly had to do it to your face. But even if they did it behind your back, it could usually be traced back to the source.

But not having any idea of who is beating you up online can leave you feeling more vulnerable. It's kind of like the classic camp-ground-horror movie: A group of kids end up in a spooky cabin in the woods. They can hear all kinds of life-threatening sounds outside, but no one knows from where the machete attack will come, so they stay stuck in a perpetual state of terror. An online machete can leave you feeling like that too. And sometimes the wounds go deeper.

Why?

So why is it that girls can be so mean? Especially since the lack of close friends seems to cause more problems for girls than boys. In fact, not being able to trust the people in your life is one of the highest predictors of anxiety in girls.[2] So why would someone push away the very thing they need most?

I've asked around to figure out why this happens, and women are perplexed—even those who were caught up in it. They look back and think, *Why did I act that way? I can't believe I treated someone that way!* It's confusing, but looking back, they were able to offer a few thoughts that might help us understand.

It boils down mostly to three main things: jealousy, insecurity, and pride.

It starts with *jealousy*. Girls can become jealous of other girls easily. She might think, *No way she's prettier than me. How is she on the homecoming court and I'm not?!*

It starts with jealousy, but that leads to the other two things: insecurity and pride.

An *insecure* girl might be acting out because of the hurt she's feeling. In fact, maybe you've heard the saying "hurting people hurt people." It's common for people who feel hurt to lash out at others in an attempt to make themselves feel better. Which leads to the last issue— pride.

Pride comes out when a girl tries to prove she's better than others. She thinks putting down the girls she's jealous of might help her feel better about herself. Messed up, I know, but that's what happens.

What to Do

So what do you do? Well, let's start with Numero Uno: you.

If you find yourself acting this way, think about the Golden Rule. In Matthew 7:12, Jesus says to treat others the way you want to be treated. Would you want others treating you the way you treat them?

Next, think about God (ooh . . . He really should have been Numero Uno). How we treat others should be a reflection of God in our lives to them. Which goes back to the characteristics of a godly woman, which we talked about in chapter 5. At the end of the day, it's much more important to honor God than to be popular.

Without a doubt, apart from illness or death in the family, dealing with mean girls is one of the hardest things teenage girls go through. So if someone is being mean to you, I'm sorry—no one should have to be treated the way you've been treated.

Start by spending some time in prayer. Share your heavy heart with God. He cares, and He will listen. And as you pray, ask God to give you wisdom in how to respond, in how to treat those who are being mean. But also ask for empathy. That girl who is being mean to you—I guarantee she's also hurting inside. Remember, *hurting people hurt people.* You never know what's going on behind the scenes in a girl's life. She may be trying to mask some really deep pain and is taking it out on you. Try performing a random act of kindness—doing something nice for her—and see what God does through that. The only person you can control is you. You can't make a mean girl be nice, but you can model the right behavior.

And don't try to handle this on your own. The devil wants you to get isolated—it's the fastest way for him to tear you down. It might seem weak to ask for help, but it's the only way you're going to get through this. So start by talking with your mom. She's probably been through this and has some ideas for you.

But also, and this is *really* important, make sure to engage teachers or principals or pastors—whoever is in a position of authority over the relationship. It's their job to help with this. And it is actually a very loving thing for you to do, because those who are bullying you might also do it to others. Let someone else fight this on your behalf. It won't be easy to ask for help, but doing nothing isn't easy either.

My neighbor's daughter said the most important thing she did was to find one true friend and bond together with that friend to protect against the mean girls. This made it easier to pull away from the crowd that was hurting her. She would still see those other girls at cheer practice or other school events, but when it came time to hang out after the game, she wouldn't join the big group. She'd peel away with her one friend who was also trying to protect herself. That strategy made a huge difference for her.

Even if you do everything you can in a perfectly God-honoring way, the other person still might not become your friend again. What's important is that you do all you can to honor God and treat others the right way. Romans 12:18 says, "If possible, so far as it depends on you, be at peace with all." There are a few important words here, like, "If possible," meaning, it's not always possible to be at peace with someone, and, "as far as it depends on you," meaning, make sure you've done what you can to make it right, because you are the only person you can control, and then leave the rest to God. He's the only One who can change the heart of the girl who is being mean to you.

Life is easier and better when you have friends around you. And if they are people who share your values and push you to grow, then you will become a better person too. So do all you can to spend time around friends that will make you better.

But also ask yourself, are you a good friend? Are you the kind of person you would want to hang out with? The best way to find a friend is to be a friend. Are you loyal and trustworthy? Think about the things you most value in a friend and start working to develop those qualities in your own life.

Though I lost a true friend this year, I've been working for years to keep some other good friendships. In college I started meeting with two guys to read through the book *Disciplines of a*

Check what's most important to you in a friendship:
- ☐ loyalty
- ☐ laughter
- ☐ shared hobbies
- ☐ similar interests
- ☐ sports
- ☐ food
- ☐ favorite games
- ☐ other:_____

Godly Man, and it had a big influence on all three of us. Since we also shared almost every class, we spent a ton of time together, which helped our friendship grow. But after college we parted ways, moving to separate states. We all wanted to stay connected, so we started doing camping trips. At first it was once every other year or so, but after having kids we turned it into an annual father-son trip. Every year it's hard to make the trip happen—all three of us are busy—but we keep making it happen because our friendships are important. When I get together with those guys, it only takes about thirty minutes of name-calling and back-slapping before we're able to go deep again because we have tons of great history.

Here's the point: If you want good friendships—and make no mistake, they are one of the most valuable things you'll have in life—then you have to work at it and fight for it. Don't give up. It is worth the effort!

10

Mentors

Mentors are people older than you, with more experience in life, who can help prepare you for what's ahead. It can be a formal relationship with clear expectations and guidelines, but it can also be informal, where you seek someone out time to time, or even from afar.

This really has been one of the defining aspects of the way I've lived life. For some reason I've always had a burning instinct to be around people older than me who I want to be like. I find a way to weasel into their world, and then extract everything possible out of them. Maybe it's because I'm always looking for shortcuts to life, or "life-hacks." If someone else can do it better, I want to know.

I've mentioned already my youth minister in high school, Kerry Jones. I did everything possible to get time around him and learn from him, even rising early to join him in the gym, or staying up late for a Bible study, or riding to school for a pre-class youth meeting. Wherever he was, I wanted to be there.

Dennis Rainey, the founder of FamilyLife, has also been a mentor to me for years. When I first heard him speak I thought, *Now that's a guy I want to work for*. I was young and willing to do grunt work just to get time around him. And you'll likely need to be willing to serve someone you admire, especially if lots of people want their time, in order to get time with them. But it's worth it.

It's really pretty simple to find a mentor. When you see someone you want to be like, do what you can to get time around them and learn from them. But you have to start by identifying them. So right now, write down the name of a person or two you admire and what it is you admire about them.

Person / Quality you admire

_____

_____

_____

_____

Informal Mentors

Now, you can also learn a ton from afar. Sometimes people you admire may have outlined their ideas in a book or video, or you might be able to learn what you need over a phone call. There's no one way to go about it, but a good rule of thumb is to start simply and work your way up: Search all you can online, then their books, then get face time, and if you still feel you haven't learned what you need, figure out how to find ongoing time around them.

Books

Books can also be mentors. In fact, books have been some of the most important mentors in my life. I mentioned how Francis

Schaeffer had a big influence on me, yet we've never met. I've only read his books. I also read books by his wife about their life together, and biographies others have written about him. Over time it kind of felt like I got to know him personally, much like an in-person mentor. Books can't replace a mentor, but they sure can help fill in some gaps.

But how do you know which books to read? Start by asking people you admire about the books that have influenced them.

Mark Hamby, founder of Lamplighter Ministries, said biographies were especially instrumental in growing his love of reading. In fact, when Mark was a young Christian, a man stepped into his life and challenged him to read a collection of short missionary biographies. That unlocked a love of reading and inspired him to launch the ministry he still leads today.[1]

You might be thinking, *Reading is old-fashioned. Video is the way to learn things these days*, or, *I'm not really a reader; I'm more of a doer*. I've heard these objections so many times I've lost count. But one thing I have noticed is that a deep hunger for spiritual growth is almost always accompanied by an intense interest in good books. I've seen it time and again; a young man or woman has hardly any interest in reading, but when he or she really begins to grow spiritually, you couldn't keep enough good books in front of them.

When I met my friend Jimmy, he told me he had hardly ever read a full book, even in college. He was more of a jock, a basketball star, and kind of took pride in *not* reading. But not long after we met he started taking his faith more seriously. Soon he was reading big, thick theological books, ones he would only have used to prop a door open just months before.

Two quotes about reading keep resonating in my head over and over again. The first showed up in the first chapter:

You'll be the same person tomorrow as you are today except for the people you meet and the books you read.

—Charles T. Jones

and

Those who choose not to read books are no better off than those who can't.

—unknown

Many great leaders of history were also great readers. Theodore Roosevelt, quite possibly the most active human ever, and still our youngest president, would read one or two *entire* books a night, even as president! If the president of the United States—who probably has more demands on his time than most—makes reading a priority, it might behoove you to take a look at some good books.

One list of recommended books that influenced me was in the back of a book I mentioned before, *Disciplines of a Godly Man*.[2] From that list, *Mere Christianity* probably had more influence in my life than any other book besides the Bible.

Take a minute to look over the lists in the back of this book and write down one of the books you'd like to start reading. Buy a copy or find it at the library today and start reading it right away—you won't be sorry!

I'm going to read this book: _____

_____

Be a Mentor

There's one more aspect to mentoring that's really important. While you're seeking people to pour into your life, make sure you're also pouring into the lives of others, that you're being a mentor to someone. I remember thinking, *But who would want me as a mentor? What do I have to offer anyone?* Well, think back to when you were twelve or thirteen. Imagine if someone your age had reached out to you and shared some of their wisdom with you. How helpful would that have been? Man, whenever a ninth-

or tenth-grader paid me any attention when I was in sixth grade, that was amazing.

An important part of the Christian life is to get your eyes off yourself and onto others. When you're too self-focused you can get in a bad place in a hurry. Your life needs to be more like "living water," where fresh water is flowing in and out, rather than a stagnant pool that smells like decaying fish and putrid pond scum. Eww.

Second Timothy 2:2 is a great verse about this: "And what you have heard from me in the presence of many witnesses entrust to faithful men, who will be able to teach others also" (ESV). Dennis Rainey modeled this well, pushing those he mentored to also be mentoring others, and then pushing those to keep the chain of mentoring going.

So how do you find someone to mentor? The first step is to see whom God has already placed around you. Who is already in your life that is just a few years younger than you? If you have younger siblings, that is the PERFECT place to start. I remember when I first realized my younger brothers looked up to me. My attitude toward them changed at that point and our relationship became much stronger. I looked for opportunities to invest in them by taking them places or having Bible studies together. We didn't have to hang out all the time—I still wanted time to hang with my friends—but I also had a new vision for how to influence their lives for good.

You can also serve at church or at a community center, library, or after-school program. What do you already love to do? Basketball? Reading? Golf? Crafts? Whatever it is, find a way to teach your skill to others.

However, I wouldn't walk up to someone and say, "I should be your mentor." That feels a little too "me" centered. Instead, ask about something specific. "Hey, do you want to join a Bible study I'm doing for a couple of girls your age?" Then just begin to pour yourself into their life. Over time you'll probably have people approach you. That's when mentoring gets exciting—when you can begin to tailor a mentoring relationship to who you are and to what the person needs.

Be praying for God to open doors for you to find a mentor and to be a mentor. I promise He'll surround you with the right people to help you become the young man or woman He is calling you to be.

11

Romance and Dating

All right, I caught you. You know who you are. You picked up this book and flipped right to this chapter, skipping over the *thousands* of other words I labored over to lead up to this. No, it's okay. Really. I'm not mad. I'M NOT!

Even if you didn't skip ahead to this chapter (*thank you*), it's pretty safe to say that you have a high level of interest in romance and dating. If you're hanging with your friends, it probably won't be long before the romance talk starts. *"I heard she likes him and he likes her. Really? No way! Yes, way!"* Love is definitely a hot topic.

Why is that? Why does almost every movie or novel have a love story running right through the middle? Seems so predictable. You'd think humanity would be bored with that formula by now. Maybe next year we'll see a spike in films with gripping mentoring sub-plots. Yeah, maybe not.

It all goes back to the way God designed the world to work. From the very first chapter of the story of creation, He brought a man and a woman together to love each other and to care for the planet as a team. And when the man saw the woman for the first time, he broke out into song and wrote a love poem extolling her beauty to the world (or, at least, to the animals). I'm guessing he even added a fist pump and a prayer of thanksgiving. God has put something inside us that longs for love. And that is a very good thing!

So what does that mean when you're a teenager? That's the big question to tackle in this chapter. How do you go about romantic relationships right now? It's not easy. In fact, I suspect most teens find the whole thing a mess. Sure, it's fun and exciting, but there's way more confusion and mishap than victory when it comes to love.

I remember the first girl I dated. Well, "dated" is a bit misleading. It was eighth grade, and about the only time we saw each other was at church. Can you really date at church? Man, was that relationship awkward. Mostly because everyone is awkward in eighth grade. It was just a big bucket full of awkwardness. I thought she was nice and cute and fun to be around, but I really had no idea what the point of the relationship was.

Part of the problem was that I had no category for dating—no framework for the purpose—so as a result, I had no idea of the purpose for it. And when you don't know what the purpose of something is, you just don't know how to approach it. Like trying to play a new board game without any instructions.

The Purpose of Dating

So what is the purpose of dating? What's the point? Dennis and Barbara Rainey, who founded what is one of the largest family ministries around, say it's pretty simple: **The purpose of dating is to find the person you want to marry.**

That's pretty straightforward. Of course, many people don't think of dating this way. I sure wasn't thinking about marrying my eighth-grade girlfriend; I could barely make a bowl of cereal for myself, let alone care for a wife! So I'm not saying you should get married in eighth grade. In fact, I don't recommend it (and I don't think most states allow it). But knowing the ultimate purpose of dating will make a huge difference in the way you approach romantic relationships at your age, and for all of life.

So how should you go about dating now in light of this purpose?

Well, before we get there, we need to talk about what is probably the biggest challenge facing you today when it comes to love and romance: our overly sexualized world.

The normal expectation for a relationship on a TV show or movie is to end up in bed together by the end of the first date. That is almost without a doubt the standard way romance is portrayed in movies and shows today. Yet there's never any hint in those shows about the risks of living this way (like STDs, pregnancy, and emotional challenges). But you don't need Hollywood to hear about teen sex. Chances are there are kids at school you know who are already having sex, so it's easy to start believing that "all the cool kids are doing it, so maybe I should too." But sex is way too powerful to be treated that casually.

A few years ago I had a chance to tour a Cold War–era nuclear missile silo. I'm a history buff, especially war history, so it was like my Disney World. (Thankfully, without life-sized mice.) Dozens of these silos were built on farmland all over the Midwest, and it is mind-blowing how much effort went into their construction. Imagine a ten-story building shoved straight down in the ground, with launch-bunkers buried alongside it one hundred feet below ground. And all of this is encased in enough concrete and steel to withstand a nuclear attack. While there, I held a piece of the scrap reinforcing steel they placed inside the concrete. It was about as thick around and as long as my forearm. This one piece probably weighed twenty-five pounds, and there were MILES of that inside the silo walls. The launch bunkers had blast doors separating each room. These doors were the size of three pickup trucks welded together and stood on end, yet they were so well designed that my six-year-old son could open and close them by hand.

So we go through the tour and end up in the launch room where I had a chance to actually throw "the switch" that could launch a nuclear missile (no worries, nothing happened). Now, here's the crazy thing I learned on the tour. After they built the silos, one of the fears the military had was when it came time to actually launch a missile, the people tasked with doing so wouldn't follow through. I mean, think about it. If you knew you were about to kill *millions* of people, would you throw the switch? It's a tough call, to say the least. So here's what they did. Every day, a few times a day, they practiced the steps of launching a missile. They would enter a series of codes they received and flip the switch—the actual switch—three times a day. The codes were never the real codes, but they appeared the same as the real codes, and the process was exactly the same. The only way they ever would have known the codes were the real thing and not just practice was if they felt the rumbling of a missile launch. The military effectively took away the difficult decision of launching a rocket of death by making it routine. They made the ability to launch the most destructive force ever created by mankind something boring and commonplace. Something routine. Something ho-hum.

The big challenge with living in an overly sexualized culture is it makes us numb to the extremely sacred nature of sex. It takes something that is so amazing, so incredibly powerful, and makes it ho-hum. And make no mistake, sex is an incredibly powerful force. I would argue there's almost nothing as powerful among the human experience, since there is no other act that has the ability to create new life. It really is mind-blowing when you think about it.

So how do we begin to restore our sense of sacredness about sex? Well, a good place to start is to examine some of the main purposes of God's design for sex.

The Purposes of Sex

There are many reasons sex exists, but I'm going to briefly mention four:

1. Procreation
2. Pleasure
3. Companionship
4. Legacy building

Procreation: From the very beginning, God brought Adam and Eve together to make more people. That's not the only purpose of sex, nor is it the highest purpose, but it is probably the most obvious.

Pleasure: Sex must be pleasurable, otherwise why would so many people want to do it? Well, it certainly can be pleasurable. Our bodies release pleasure-inducing chemicals into the brain during intercourse. Some religions have shunned pleasure in sexual intimacy, saying it's not something we're supposed to enjoy. But given that there's an entire book of the Bible dedicated to pleasure in sexual intimacy (suddenly interested in reading the Bible?), I think it's pretty easy to make a case for it.

Now, sex isn't always pleasurable. In fact, plenty of people have had only bad sexual experiences. Sex can lead to much pain and confusion in a person's life, especially given how sex is treated so casually in today's world. But by design, and done according to God's plan, sex was meant to be pleasurable.

Companionship: Just as there are chemicals released in the brain during sex for pleasure, there are also chemicals designed to bond you to another person. God designed sex so that two people really do become one—they unite in body and soul. And this is good. Because if two people procreate, then it's good to bond together and raise those children *together*. But a person with multiple sexual partners learns to break those deep attachments in order to reattach to another person. So they repeat a deeply damaging cycle—attach/ detach, attach/detach, attach/detach—over and over again. So the ability to bond with another person gets increasingly difficult. Like with a Post-it Note, the more times you use it, the less sticky it becomes. And eventually it won't stick at all. This doesn't mean a person who has had multiple sexual partners is unredeemable or less of a person, but it does mean they'll face some real challenges when it comes to emotional intimacy and commitment.

Legacy Building: The fourth reason is similar to the first, but it takes us beyond just mere procreation. Almost any man and woman can have sex and procreate and bring a child into the world. But the goal of procreation is not just to make children, but to build families and lasting legacies of godliness that help change the world.

The Bible is pretty clear that when two people love each other in marriage, it shows the world something about God's love for His people (see Ephesians 5). So when two parents practice commitment, forgiveness, kindness, and patience, when they genuinely love one another, then their children will learn what God's love is like.

All of this helps us understand why sex is so powerful. It's not just a physical act between two people with a strong attraction to each other—it has so much more meaning and significance than that. When a man and woman come together in marriage and they are absolutely committed to each other and believe their marriage is part of God's plan for the world, then they will think differently about their purpose. They'll think differently about their children. They'll think differently about their legacy. They'll have a vision for raising children who follow God and honor Him with their lives. And a God-honoring view of sex is a big part of that kind of vision.

All that might feel a bit overwhelming. So how does this understanding of sex inform the way we view dating?

Back to Dating

I hope that this grand vision of sex and marriage helps you start to see that dating and sex and marriage are not just about you. It's not just about your personal happiness. Of course, I want you to be happy and find true love! Some of the greatest joy in my life has happened in marriage. But make no mistake—and this is so, so important, yet few people ever really understand this—true happiness is a *result*, not the *purpose* of dating and marriage. This is ridiculously important. Please don't miss this. **True happiness is the *result*, not the *purpose* of dating and marriage.** If you get this flipped around, you'll end up making the relationship all about you. And you'll see your spouse or boyfriend/girlfriend as merely a means to your happiness. And boy does that lead to all kinds of problems.

True happiness will only come when you strive to date in a way that honors God. No one does it perfectly. Everyone makes mistakes because we're full of selfishness—we're all inherently self-centered at our very core. But if you strive to honor God in dating, you'll start to experience the joy He intends for you.

So how should you go about dating? Start by knowing what dating shouldn't be.

The Myth of the "Dating Relationship"

There's a great book that you should read (after you finish this one, of course) called *Sex, Dating, and Relationships*. In the book, the authors try to debunk the myth of the "dating relationship." They say that there are three God-ordained categories of male-female relationships: **Family** (father, mother, brother, sister, etc.), **Neighbor**, and **Marriage**. They say that you need to view every male-female relationship in light of one of those three categories. And in two of the three, sexual activity is prohibited (neighbor/family).

The problem with modern dating is that we've created a fourth category of relationship: the dating relationship. Dating used to be merely an activity, but now it's become a new category of relationship. And all kinds of problems come from this. Here's how it's described in *Sex, Dating, and Relationships*:

Two people who are dating appear in many ways to have a real and established relationship. They may have a title for their significant other (boyfriend or girlfriend). They are expected to remember anniversaries, holidays, and birthdays. They place upon each other certain obligations and restrictions regarding who they can and cannot spend time with. On the surface, this gives an impression of commitment, but is the commitment of a dating relationship really a commitment of any substance?[1]

They argue that a dating commitment—the shared agreement to date exclusively—is not really a commitment since either person is free to end the commitment at any time. But since the dating relationship feels like a semi-marriage, with all the markings of real commitment, then break-ups feel like a semi-divorce. And after you've gone through a number of dating relationships, you start to face the same challenge a person with multiple sexual partners has had (even if you've never had sex), like that Post-it Note that won't stick anymore.

The other thing a dating relationship confuses is physical boundaries. It's the age-old question of "how far is too far?" I remember being at a conference when a guy next to me asked that question during the Q&A time. The presenter responded, "The fact that you are asking that tells me you're probably wanting to push the boundaries." Ouch. But the questioner kept pressing him (thus proving the point). So the presenter said, "You really want to know how far is too far? Whenever you get an erection, you've gone too far." This was an audience of boys and girls. The crowd went absolutely silent. It was really awkward. Maybe the presenter had gone too far. But here's what he was trying to help this young guy see: If you're involved in any activity that arouses you sexually, you've gone too far. This was pretty eye-opening for me. Physical boundaries had always seemed a little subjective—I mean, as long as everyone kept their clothes on. But within those boundaries, it seemed like personal preference. But his assertion was that any activity that aroused you sexually was considered "sexual activity."

Here's one way I've heard it explained.[2] Let's go back to the three categories of male-female relationships in the Bible. There's a type of kiss that would be appropriate in all three relationships. In fact, in some cultures, men who are good friends will greet one another with a quick peck on the cheek. Some will even hold hands (I've seen this in Africa). I guess it's kind of like a bro hug—though a bro hug requires some serious back slapping to stay manly. So maybe a kiss with a slap would be acceptable. Let's not find out. Either way, there's a kiss that's acceptable among family and neighbors, even close friends.

However, there's another type of kiss that's acceptable in marriage but would NEVER be acceptable between a brother and sister or parent and child. In fact, just the thought of a French kiss with your brother or sister would make you want to throw up. And it should! Why? Because a French kiss—sticking your tongue in another person's mouth—is an inherently sexual kiss. A kiss like that is meant to stir up sexual feelings. Thus, that kind of kiss should be reserved for marriage, because sexual activity was only meant to occur in marriage. But modern dating relationships have created a new category of male-female relationships where sexual activity is acceptable, even among Christians, and even understood as a requirement of the relationship.

I know, you might be thinking this is crazy talk, but keep thinking about it. And as you think about it, make sure you are coming at it from a biblical perspective, not just based on how you feel.

It's really important to think about this because you need to make up your mind in advance about what are appropriate physical boundaries—before you get into a tempting situation. When hormones and emotions are charging like a bull trying to rip the head off a carpet-waving matador, that's not the time to decide. You won't have much luck getting that bovine impulse under control.

When I was dating my future wife, Julie, we would often spend time kissing and hugging. We kept our hands to ourselves but definitely enjoyed some kissing. I was serving as a counselor at a camp one summer when the guy brushing his teeth next to me shared that he and his future wife had committed to never kiss on the lips until marriage. I thought the dude was insane. I stepped back to give room for the orderlies to rush in and cart him off in a straightjacket. But no one appeared. And we kept brushing our teeth. But this idea started gnawing at me. He had set a high standard of purity to protect the young lady he loved—from his own raging hormones—and to honor her and treat her as Christ would. As the summer went along, the more the wisdom of such a decision became clear, and by the end of the camp I had made the same commitment.

It's a tall order, and it seems countercultural, but that's because *it is*. Because purity is countercultural. But it's worth it. It really is. It's the path to experiencing romance, dating, and eventually marriage, as God designed, which will lead to the utmost joy.

So what do you do? How do you approach dating, or dates, or whatever you want to call it? And how do you keep marriage in mind while you date without making every conversation too serious, without thinking every person you say "hi" to and toss a smile might be your future spouse? (*That* could drive you crazy.)

Here are seven tips to help you succeed at dating now:

1. Become the person you want to marry.

If you want to marry someone who is kind, hardworking, smart, funny, in good shape, thoughtful, and would make a great parent, then you should focus on becoming that kind of person. Like attracts like, so if you have those attributes, you're most likely to attract that kind of person. I'd encourage you to make a future-spouse must-have list and start becoming that kind of person now. One lesson I've learned in marriage and that I often tell others is that you can only control and change yourself. You won't be able to control or change your spouse. But you can influence them, and the best way to do that is leading by example. So start leading by bettering yourself now. As you grow in character, God will bring more people around you who have similar interests and character.

Here is a list of attributes that you might like. Check as many as you would like in your spouse, then rank your top 5. Now pick two you want to work on in yourself.

- ☐ smart
- ☐ funny
- ☐ hardworking
- ☐ stylish
- ☐ faithful
- ☐ compassionate
- ☐ driven
- ☐ serious about growing spiritually
- ☐ disciplined
- ☐ great family
- ☐ athletic
- ☐ musical
- ☐ loves to read church history[3]
- ☐ integrity
- ☐ other:_____

2. Don't compromise the essentials.

As you make your list, make sure that at the top of the list is *Christian*. And not Christian in name only, but someone who has a genuine relationship with Jesus. They should consider Jesus to be the most important person in their life. The Bible should be their ultimate authority, and they should be actively growing spiritually.

I once heard Pastor Tommy Nelson explain to a group of college guys why this is so important. (I'm paraphrasing): "Men, if your wife will not submit to the authority of Scripture, then how in the world will you expect her to follow your leadership? What will you do if she won't follow you? Will you beat her? Of course not! That won't endear her to you. No, there has to be a higher authority to direct her, because you're going to let her down. You will. And the only hope you have of your relationship growing and flourishing is if you both submit yourselves to the authority of God's Word." Strong statement, but it's true. If you aren't on the same page about the thing that is most central to your identity, then there will be a chasm to cross in almost every decision you face. You'll be coming from completely different worldviews at almost every turn, and that rarely turns out well. That's what the Bible calls "unequally yoked" in 2 Corinthians 6:14 (ESV).

This is why it's important not to "missionary date." I've seen it too many times. A Christian girl tries to date a non-Christian guy to lead him closer to Jesus. It almost never works. In many situations, the girl (or guy) ends up compromising their own beliefs to accommodate the person they were trying to influence. Again, you can't change someone else; only God can change him or her. Don't ever risk compromising your faith for a romantic relationship.

3. Pursue friendship first.

Want to see if someone is good marriage material? Get to know them as a friend first. See how they act around others. Spend time with them in groups. Get to know their friends. See what makes them sad, happy, and mad. Are they easily irritated? What happens when you disagree? Do they rejoice when others win, or do they throw a fit when they lose? You can see all this when you hang out in friend groups. Friendship really is one of the most important parts of a successful marriage. All the things that are true of a good friend are also true of a marriage, so you'll be way down the road toward a successful romantic relationship if you learn to be a good friend first.

4. Get to know their family.

It's hard to believe, but a marriage is in many ways the merging of two families. Even if you live far from your parents after marriage, each of you is carrying buckets of your parents into marriage. So try to find ways to hang out around their family. Watch how they interact. Do they talk about problems, or stuff them? Are they kind to each other, or harsh? How does he treat his mom? Or how does she treat her dad? These observations will give you clues about how they will treat you. And finally, if things do go wrong between you and this person, well, it will be a lot harder to treat them poorly if you know their parents and siblings and if they know you. That helps protect everyone. One of my brothers did this well with a girl he dated in high school. Her dad even became friends with my dad and me through the process. The men still keep in touch to this day, with no shame or hard feelings hanging over the relationship, even though my brother ended up marrying someone else.

5. Be intentional!

I've seen so many folks just float through relationships with very little intentionality, without a clear plan. That will fly in eighth grade (though still not best), but mature people don't treat others this way. They don't string someone along, keeping them guessing about their intentions. That's a waste of everyone's time. This is especially important for guys, since I believe God designed men to be the initiator in the relationship. In fact, it was always an immediate *no* for me if a girl asked me out.

Girls—think about it this way: Do you really want to be married to a guy who wouldn't put forth the effort to initiate with you? That's a passive guy. And I can guarantee that if your man is passive, you will have *all kinds* of problems after marriage.

There are ways you can still show interest without taking the lead—ask your mom for help with that, or other women you respect—but I promise, you want a guy who will initiate and take the lead. You are valuable enough to have a guy pursue you.

6. Be accountable.

Make sure your life is transparent and an open book for people you trust to gain access. Sin is like black mold. It grows in dark, hidden places. But if you bring it out into the light—where people can see it—then it dies. So when I was dating Julie, we wouldn't be alone in places together where others couldn't quickly check on us. Or if my parents were out of town, she didn't come over to my house; instead, we met out at a restaurant or coffee shop—somewhere in public. Set boundaries that honor the relationship and protect your emotional and physical purity. Guys, take the lead on this. Don't be passive-aggressive and make the girl say no.

Keep your relationships out in the open, where people you trust can see them and give feedback. Ask men and women you trust to give you feedback. This is a HUGE skill to develop now, because you'll need accountability your entire life.

7. Read a ton. Read, read, read to gain insight from the wisdom of others. Here's a few books I recommend:

- *I Kissed Dating Goodbye* by Joshua Harris
- *Passion and Purity* by Elisabeth Elliot
- *Lady in Waiting* by Jackie Kendall and Debby Jones (written for girls, but guys should read it too)
- *Sex, Dating, and Relationships* by Gerald Hiestand and Jay Thomas
- *The Meaning of Marriage* by Tim Keller

Why is all of this important? Because developing God-honoring romantic relationships is a skill. It takes time and hard work, but if done right, it can be one of the greatest joys of your life. If done wrong, it can be one of the hardest things you go through.

Story Time

Mary and Jim (not their real names) met at camp one summer when they were both teenagers. They lived in different parts of the country, so they decided to keep in touch by writing when they went back home. Mary had been praying for a friend, and

Jim quickly became an answer to her prayer. In fact, he was her first best friend. Being deep thinkers, they were able to connect on a more intense level than with anyone their age before. Jim was charming and nice and would compliment Mary, something she hadn't experienced from guys her age. And Mary was funny and kind and full of encouragement, which Jim often needed.

Not too long after that summer, even though separated by hundreds of miles, they became boyfriend and girlfriend. Things were great for a while, but then they began to argue. They would have a disagreement and not talk for days. Then Jim would lash out, but later tell Mary it wasn't her fault, which left her confused.

Eventually Jim, a year older than Mary, started his first year of college. His school was near Mary's hometown, so he was able to visit more often. But the face time didn't improve things. In fact, more time together meant more time to argue. For instance, Jim had roomed with a guy pursuing a very different lifestyle. Mary didn't agree with this and felt he wasn't listening to her. But he felt like she was being controlling and not trusting him to do the right thing.

Being in-person also brought new struggles. Jim started to push Mary toward a level of physical involvement that she wasn't comfortable with. At first she said no, but then started giving in little by little. Even though she knew this was wrong, she felt stuck. She had invested two years of her life into the relationship at this point. She thought they would get married someday. So she reasoned it would be all right to give in a little if it made things better.

Mary's friends knew something wasn't right. They could see she was changing. Her normal cheery disposition was now weighed down by the strain of the relationship. Her parents were also down on Jim by this point.

They all told her to break up with Jim, but she didn't want to hear it. Mary thought, *They just don't know the real Jim.* She became angry, said it wasn't their business. They backed off, knowing that pressing Mary to break up with Jim would probably backfire. She started lying to everybody, telling them everything was fine.

Mary was sure that sticking it out and suffering a little bit would bring back the Jim she knew. Somehow, God would honor her struggle and make them live happily ever after.

Jim was becoming more vocal about his dislike for Mary's friends and family. So to save the relationship with Jim, she withdrew from them. And the physical advances continued, making her more and more uncomfortable, even feeling violated and used.

The disconnection from her family weighed heavily on her. She was isolated, unhappy, probably even depressed. But she couldn't break away from Jim. At this point, so much of her identity was wrapped up in him. When they met, she had just been through an identity crisis, and as she rebuilt her identity, Jim was with her every step of the way. So she came to equate her identity and significance with Jim. She couldn't imagine life without him.

She was miserable and didn't know what to do.

So for the first time in a long time, she began to pray. And very quickly she had hope and direction from God: If Jim wouldn't respect her boundaries, she would break it off. Mary told Jim how she was feeling. In response, he wrote a long letter, sharing many things he didn't like about her. The letter hurt, but she finally saw how Jim was turning her strengths into flaws in order to manipulate her.

She called her mom for the first time in a while to get perspective. And then she broke up with Jim the very next day.

He tried to blame her: She wasn't doing enough, wasn't taking enough interest in him and his life. But she had been trying *so hard* to make it work and had been putting *so much* effort into being interested in things he liked. It was another confirmation she was making the right choice.

It took a while to realize she had been in an abusive relationship. Looking back, Mary can see the red flags. First, Jim kept surrounding himself with people without good values, and that changed him over time. Second, Jim isolated Mary from her friends and family. He would subtly undermine their love for her and their influence in her life, criticizing them behind their backs, and setting himself up to control the relationship. And how they handled conflict was a mess. When arguing, Jim would often turn from the issue to attacking Mary and her character. This pushed her further into isolation and withdrawal.

Lastly, and this is a big one, she wishes she would have had a much stronger sense of self-respect. She didn't talk much with her parents about sexuality—it felt too taboo—and had not developed a strong sense of personal value. For some reason she thought it was normal for a guy to try to push past her boundaries, and that it's the woman's job to defend herself. But now she knows she *should* expect a man to respect her, and that she *is* worth respecting.

Mary wonders now what God has in store for her. It's been a while since she broke things off with Jim, and she's beginning to heal. She knows now that God loves her and wants what's best for her. She knows she needs to stay in the community and not get isolated from her friends and family, and not compromise her values. And best of all, she's reconnecting with God, pursuing Him and not letting that relationship drift. She knows prayer is critical to the success of any relationship.

Ultimately Mary was able to break up with Jim through understanding what was core to her identity. At first she let her sense of identity get too wrapped up with Jim. But as her awareness of her true identity grew, like her faith, friends, and family, she was able to see what was happening with Jim more clearly.

Love and Identity

What Mary realized at the end of her relationship with Jim is so critical. You can't get the most out of any relationship unless you've rooted your life in something stronger than that relationship, a lasting identity. Otherwise, if that relationship crumbles, your identity will crumble.

Guys and girls both need to be careful with how to treat a young lady or young man. You can't just manipulate them to your own needs, to get what only you want out of a relationship. That's not sacrificial love, that's self-love.

Jim put Mary in a relational vacuum, but I've seen girls do this to guys as well. It happened with a buddy of mine. I watched him pull away from some of his closest friends because of a girl. She isolated him from his friends because she was threatened by the depth of his friendships. She thought she couldn't compete with that. It's a shame, because his friends were great guys who helped make him a better person. And he gave them up for her. And then later she ditched him.

You've probably seen this, haven't you? The couple who totally ignores their friends and latches on to each other like two leeches. They seemingly disappear from the face of the earth. But then things fall apart and lo and behold, your friend is back! You never went anywhere, but they sure left the planet for a moon phase or two.

Why is it people get so caught up in a relationship like that? Are they afraid of getting stuck on a single boat in a sea of exclusivity? How can we let something like that radically alter our life? I promise, you are better off being single than in a relationship that slowly sucks the life out of you. It's like a virus on your computer killing the processing power. Who wants that?

In a real relationship, one full of genuine love, both people grow. Both flourish. Both become better versions of themselves. You don't have to make someone smaller to make yourself feel better. If you do that, you're actually bringing both persons down. Instead, get around those who make you a better version of yourself. That is genuine love.

Let Love Be Genuine

Romans 12:9–10 is a great passage for thinking rightly about relationships: "Let love be genuine. Abhor what is evil; hold fast to what is good. Love one another with brotherly affection. Outdo one another in showing honor" (ESV). The key word in these verses, and the one that really stands out in our world today, is *genuine*.

I severely dislike buying belts; it takes forever to find the right one because there are two kinds of belts. One is shiny and black, looks expensive but doesn't break the bank, but only lasts about a year. It will snap in two right when you need your pants the most, like walking in the door to meet the parents of your Friday night date. Not a good first impression.

The other kind of belt isn't flashy, but it's thick, durable, and smells like a boot factory. Sure, it costs half your paycheck, but it could be the last belt you buy. You might even pass it down to your grandchildren. It can also be used in emergencies to carry books, climb a tree, or lash a bowie knife to a stick to fend off a flurry of rabid squirrels.

What's the difference? *Genuine* leather. The second comes right off the back of the cow. It's tough because it's been through some harsh winters and still kept the cow warm. But the first belt is some combination of recycled taillight fragments, flax seed husks, and melted crayons. That's great for craft time at vacation Bible school, but not for protecting your legs from UV rays.

This world is full of fake things masquerading as the real thing. But the fake things are a temporary substitute, failing under pressure, not lasting when you need them to hold up. That's why we need *genuine love*. Fake love is everywhere. Just this morning, you probably said (with great enthusiasm) something like, "I *LOVE* Cap'N Crunch!" Yes, that is a certain type of love, but will Cap'N Crunch stand by you when times get tough? I think not. Genuine love endures, stands firm, holds fast to what is good, and seeks to do the right thing, even when times are tough. Even when feelings fade.

The challenge for you, and for me, is will you be genuine? Will you love others with a genuine love? That's what every human wants. Don't offer fake love to others. Buy a genuine belt, keep your pants up, and show genuine love and concern for those who are around you. Your family, your friends, and yes, even your enemies will thank you.[4]

So that's romantic relationships with the opposite sex. But what do you do if you feel a romantic attraction to someone of the same sex? Well, our next chapter will talk about that.

12

Same-Sex Attraction

Sam didn't grow up as a Christian. In fact, it wasn't until late in high school that he became close friends with some guys at work who invited him to church, where he began investigating the message of Jesus. This was an intriguing and exciting time for him, but also confusing, because Christianity wasn't the only new idea he was wrestling with.

Sam was also coming into the realization that he was attracted to men more than women. He'd had a few girlfriends up to this point, but he'd always felt more of a connection with some of his close guy friends. So he began to wonder, *Am I gay?* and he also wondered, *How do these feelings match up with being a Christian?*

Sam did put his faith in Christ and now is a pastor. He still experiences same-sex attractions, though he has never acted on them, and he has remained single to this day.

So what's a guy like Sam to do? Or maybe a young lady who feels some of these things, like Rosaria, whose story you'll read later in this chapter.

Same-sex attraction is a pretty big topic these days. But there's a ton of confusion and emotion swirling around the issue. Opinions seem to change all the time. Every year prominent public figures, politicians, and even a few high-profile pastors turn from opposing gay marriage to supporting it. And the labels for those who are same-sex attracted keep changing and expanding all the time. It's hard to keep up with the right terms to avoid offense.

My hope in this chapter is to give some bearings on the topic, some rails that will help guide the runaway train of emotion that has often characterized these discussions. There are certainly some things about same-sex attraction that are murky and confusing, yet there are some aspects that are easier to understand.

Part of the confusion is due to the upheaval our entire culture is facing on this issue. Just as how our understanding of what it means to be a man or a woman can be heavily shaped by the culture, so it is with the acceptability—or unacceptability—of same-sex attraction. Our world encourages young people to experiment with whatever attractions one feels. The popular message declares this to be the path of discovery for finding the "real you" and coming into one's "true identity." Thus, the popular conclusion for a person experiencing same-sex attraction is that they must be gay, and to dare question that identity is to deny the very core of who you are.

But should your attractions have that much of a role in defining you? Should they play that big of a part in your identity? My guess is that most people have plenty of things that grab their attention and emotions that they don't necessarily want to be defined by.

So how can we gain some perspective on this?

Well, as we've done throughout this book, let's start by looking at what the Bible says. That's no small task, though. There have been dozens and dozens of books written from both sides of the coin. So many points and counterpoints could be made—are you getting tired already? To avoid getting overwhelmed, let's focus on a couple of big ideas, and then share thoughts on how to live in light of these truths, both in your own life and relating to others who struggle with same-sex attraction.

First: The Big Picture of the Bible

A pretty important starting point is to contemplate same-sex attraction in light of one of the main themes of the Bible. It has always fascinated me how the Bible is bookended by marriage. *In the beginning* God brings a man and a woman together (that's the "naked and unashamed" part). He takes a babe and a dude and says, "Go start the world." And their marriage, their life together, sets the pattern for all civilization to come (no pressure there, Adam and Eve).

But the Bible also *ends* with a marriage. And this marriage is the culmination of the first marriage. This marriage celebration is about restoring the world to God's plan. And at the wedding reception, God brings together the bride (the church) and finally unites her with Jesus at the marriage supper of the Lamb.

What does this have to do with same-sex attraction? From the beginning of history, all throughout time, and at the end of the age, God's design was that marriage between a man and a woman might serve as a picture of Christ's relationship with the Church. There is something about the differences between man and woman that tells us about God's love for His people. This vision for marriage sets the stage for how we should think about sex, romance, and marriage.

Second: Consider the Clear Message of the Bible

In every instance where the Bible mentions homosexuality (or indeed any kind of sex outside of marriage), it is always spoken of negatively. The overwhelming message of the Bible around sexual attraction is centered on affirming God's design for a man and a woman to come together and experience intimacy in marriage. Yes, the meaning of some ancient words and historical setting and specific passages can be discussed and debated, but it still doesn't offset the balance of the main emphasis of Scripture when it comes to sexuality.

So any kind of sex that occurs outside of a biblical marriage, one between a man and a woman, is clearly prohibited in the Bible. Some will choose to reject the Bible in light of this, to no longer hold it as authoritative because of how this feels. I get that. This can be a hard thing to consider, especially if you or someone you really love and care about is wrestling with same-sex attraction. But hang with me—don't toss aside the Bible and its relevance yet. In fact, there's no more relevant message to apply to this struggle than the healing and redeeming power of Christ. The Bible doesn't treat sexual struggles as some special class of sin. You can apply the message of the Bible the same as any other challenge.

And here are six reasons why:

1. The Bible teaches that all Christians are to practice restraint in some areas of life.

When Sam first began to wrestle with his attraction toward men and what that meant as a new Christian, he also understood that sacrifice and restraint are an essential practice for the Christian life. Sam had this to say about our attractions:

> All of us experience feelings that are part of . . . a sinful world. We're all fallen. [But] we're not meant to act on all of those feelings. A key part of maturity, as a man [or woman], and as a Christian is learning how to say no to some of our feelings. That's a discipline we all have to go through. It's something the Lord Jesus would've had to face as He experienced temptation and had to grow in His own obedience to His Heavenly Father. So we need to be very discerning with what the culture around us has to say and make sure we know what the Scriptures say.[1]

I remember hearing Tommy Nelson, one of my favorite Bible teachers, talk about his struggle with anger. There were times he would be boiling with rage. He just wanted to grab an ax handle and beat the holy inferno out of a church member (in love, of course). But even he agreed that's not a feeling a Christian should pursue. He had to trust God to give him the strength to deny his feelings in that moment.

2. You are not simply the sum of your attractions.

Society wants to make your sexual attractions the center of your identity, but that shouldn't be the case for anyone, regardless of who you are attracted to. Yes, our sexuality is a big part of our identity, but it's certainly not the most important part. A healthy person sees their identity as far too complex and important to be defined by any one category. You don't just add up attractions to define a person. And the presence of an attraction does not require that you act upon it.

3. Sex is not the ultimate basis of your identity.

Sam was able to trust Christ to help him rightly understand his sexual attractions because he understood that Christ had to be at the center of his identity. Again, Sam shared,

> I had learned to trust the Bible on so many issues, so that when I began to understand what the Bible said about homosexuality, though that was a hard teaching to receive, I knew I could trust the Bible. . . . We're told in Genesis 1, "God created them male and female." So He didn't create us same-sex attracted or opposite-sex attracted. Our human identity comes from our bodily gender, rather than from the sexual attractions we experience.[2]

4. Sexual attractions often change.

Our feelings, our attractions, can be pretty unpredictable in our teen years. Sam had friends that felt same-sex attracted as teens but who later grew out of those feelings. It happens fairly often, because sexual attractions tend to be fluid for a young person. You might feel a very strong attraction to a person of the same sex when you're fifteen, but that feeling might fade before you reach adulthood. In fact, just about *every* fifteen-year-old feeling is susceptible to change. I remember being completely enamored with a girl at that age, and yet I can see now that I was not thinking clearly. I also liked the Christian heavy-metal band Stryper (don't judge me), further evidence of my temporary insanity.

Another caution I have for you during these years: Be careful not to equate an attraction to a *person* with an attraction to an *entire sex*. You may just be feeling a strong affinity with an individual rather than an entire sex. Either way, know that feelings may, and likely will, change over time.

5. Don't go it alone.

Feelings may fade over time, but for many people, like Sam, same-sex attraction might never completely go away. If this is an area where you struggle, find someone you can trust and talk with. I know it is risky—so you'll want to choose wisely—but keeping things stuffed inside is risky as well. Confide in those who can help give you a bigger perspective. Some of your peers may be helpful, and some may not. But you also need adults you can trust who have time and perspective on their side. Sam found great help in talking with others about his struggles. He said, "I was very anxious about sharing this with other people. I had sort of an irrational fear, in hindsight, that I would lose friends. And in fact, it was an overwhelmingly positive experience to share it."

Now, I've heard enough stories to know that not everyone has a positive experience like Sam, so tread carefully. But one other caution: Don't "confide" with the person you're attracted to. That's just a cheap way of telling them you like them and making it seem spiritual. And it's way too self-serving. That's the last person you want to confide in about this. But make sure to build a community around you who can help you process. Find people who will truly "Bear one another's burdens" (Galatians 6:2), and "Weep with those who weep" (Romans 12:15).

6. Don't believe the hype.

Right now, in our world, the applause goes to the "brave" person who comes out and embraces their same-sex attractions. However, though it's not applauded, not even a golf clap, there's also a great deal of bravery involved in wrestling with your emotions. Don't fall into the trap of believing everything will be better if you simply give yourself over to whatever you're feeling. Happiness is never that simple. I'm always skeptical of a belief system that makes perfect peace and affluence, or health and wealth, seem simple to attain. That's a pretty shallow view of joy.

We live in an age where happiness and affluence have become ultimate—they have become gods that must be served. Yet they are false gods. Happiness is not the goal; rather, it is the *result* of life centered in Christ. It's the result of wise living, not an end unto itself.

So those are some ideas for how to think about same-sex attraction if you're struggling with it personally. But what do you do if you're not struggling but have a friend who is? How can you best encourage them and relate to them?

How to Relate to a Person's Same-Sex Attraction

Start with love. If someone who wrestles with this has confided in you, show love. They must trust you enough to tell you something like this, so don't beat them up or create distance. Stay in their world and keep loving them, keep supporting them, keep befriending and helping them find wise counsel. And keep in mind they may have already experienced some deep hurt from others. So come with an attitude of compassion and care.

Speak the truth in love. In the midst of staying connected and encouraging, it's okay to continue to stand for truth—for a biblical view of sexuality. But make sure you present truth in a way that is receivable. Start with listening. I know I'm much more likely to receive truth when it is shared in love. A friend of mine came to me after feeling I had betrayed him. But he was kind—and not accusatory—as he explained the situation in a way that made me more open to hearing his side. That exchange has stuck with me and made me a better friend. You can disagree with yet still respect a person. In fact, sometimes disagreeing is the most loving thing you can do. To remain silent while a true friend goes down a path that strays from biblical truth is the opposite of love.

Rosaria's Story

Rosaria[3] also experienced same-sex attraction as a young person, but it wasn't until she turned twenty-eight that she came out as a lesbian. She was hired by Syracuse University to build their Gay and Lesbian studies program, and she was happy. She loved what she did and she loved the person she lived with. She wasn't a Christian, and she wasn't looking for Jesus. In fact, she wasn't really looking for anything.

But one day she began a research project that involved reading through the Bible. She tackled it like any other project, poring over Scripture for up to five hours a day. But she had loads of questions, so she started meeting with a pastor and his wife over dinner. They were kind and thoughtful and engaged with her, even over her most difficult objections, and never judged her lifestyle. This went on for a while—over a year—till one day the pastor said he thought God was pursuing Rosaria and that she was going to have to make a decision soon about what she believed about the Bible. Not too long after that she found herself praying that God would help her "to be a godly woman." She even laughed out loud thinking how absurd it sounded coming from someone like her. But Christ had entered her life and begun a change, especially to her identity. She said, "[At first] I felt the same. I still felt like a lesbian. But what didn't feel the same was my identity. It was clear to me in Scripture that a true believer had to have an identity rooted in Christ."[4]

As a same-sex-attracted Christian, Rosaria's life took a different turn than Sam's. Her attractions slowly changed. She eventually married a man, gave up her position at Syracuse, and is now a homeschooling mom. And yes, even she chuckles at how that sounds. What a big change!

She followed a different path than Sam, but they both had to trust Christ to guide them through their same-sex attractions. And when it comes to figuring out what this means for you, Rosaria had this to say:

> Find a group of safe, godly people—your parents, your pastor, some friends at church—and really let them know how you feel. But don't make an identity [out of your attractions]. Because any identity that is apart from Christ becomes a place where we start to doubt God's goodness.

Rosaria and Sam both found their ultimate significance, their true identity, not in their sexual attractions but in Christ. And they rooted that identity in Him by trusting His word to be true and to be the guide and authority. That is my main hope for you as you read this book—that whatever challenge or question or struggle you're facing in life, you're able to trust it to Christ—to depend on Him for wisdom and direction no matter how daunting it may seem.

MISSIONAL IDENTITY

A BRIGHT FUTURE

I'm a huge fan of C. S. Lewis. He wrote all the CHRONICLES OF NARNIA books, like *The Lion, the Witch and the Wardrobe*. I read those as a boy, and then discovered his other books in high school and college.

One day I was reading through *Surprised by Joy*, an autobiography mostly about his childhood, and had a surprising moment of my own. In the book he tells of his infatuation with literature, poetry, and writing. His young imagination would run wild, creating characters and languages with his brother. He even wrote his first story at seven years old. It was a boyhood of dreams, like an eternal picnic in the family garden.

But then his mother passed away and he was shipped off to boarding school, which he later described as more dreadful than the trenches of World War I. He noticed pretty quickly that the athletic boys were the most popular. But with no athletic bone in his frame, Lewis gladly traded the ball field turf for the pages of his favorite classics. And it was his love of ancient languages and myths and epic stories that led to his tremendous literary output.

C. S. Lewis's books have sold some 200 million copies; the movies based on THE CHRONICLES OF NARNIA have grossed over $1.5 billion, his textbooks are still used in top universities today, and his book *Mere Christianity* (my favorite) is often cited as one of the most influential Christian books of our era. That's one successful dude.

But what if Lewis, as a young, unathletic boy in boarding school, would have rejected his love for literature, his love for writing and languages, to pursue acceptance? What if he would have given up Homer and Milton and Virgil to focus on his cricket game? We might never have had Narnia, or the space trilogy, or *Mere Christianity*—books that have changed so many lives.

And so I began to think about myself and wonder, *How am I trusting God to use the gifts and talents He's given me?* Even if those aren't the things that make someone "popular." He's given me certain gifts for a reason, things that I'm decent at and enjoy. After reading *Surprised by Joy*, I really began to delight in how God made me for the first time. Because—and please don't tell anyone else this—I can be a bit quirky at times. It's true! And yes, I know you can be too. But sometimes it's those quirky things, like making up your own alphabet, or whatever you find fascinating but fear others might make fun of, that make you most interesting. By the way, J.R.R. Tolkien, a close friend of Lewis, made up languages. And that led him to write THE LORD OF THE RINGS—also a ridiculously successful series of books, and now movies.

So what about you? What "Narnias" are lurking within you? Maybe you won't be the next C. S. Lewis, but there is something God has in store for you that He wants you to embrace. How has

He uniquely wired you as a person? Not just mimicking others, but discovering *your* gifts. What is your mission in life—and how is that a part of your identity as an individual? And how do you figure that out? That's what the next couple of chapters are about.

13

The Age of Opportunity and Road Hazards

God has amazing things for you in this season of life. This can be an incredible "age of opportunity." But beware: Some things can take you off course and distract you from the awesome life God has for you. But here's something even more exciting: You don't have to wait ten years to start figuring this out. These years RIGHT NOW are some of the most exciting in your life for learning who you are and trying great things.

The Age of Opportunity

I love how the author Paul Tripp calls this season "the age of opportunity." He says that many teens get stuck in the mind-set that it's a really hard stage that you just have to survive somehow and get through with enough sanity to stumble out of your parents' house when you turn eighteen.

But that couldn't be further from the truth. You'll face challenges for sure, but Tripp says, "These are years of unique opportunity. Greater responsibility, wider geography, wider circle of friends and responsibilities. It's a time of wonderful, wonderful opportunity."[1]

I couldn't agree more. You can accomplish so much because of your energy, your youth, your creativity, and your enthusiasm for life. One of my favorite verses for teens is, "Don't let anyone look down on you because you are young, but set an example for the believers" (1 Timothy 4:12 NIV). You have a great advantage and gift as a young person to inspire those who are older than you. I promise, you really can. There are few things as encouraging to me than seeing teens getting after it, making the most of life. It makes me want to step up my game.

My son right now—he's in seventh grade—is working hard at school, making A's, swimming competitively, reading good books, and he also runs a lawn-mowing business in the summers. His energy and drive are so motivating. Not just to me, but to many other adults who hear of his endeavors. And he's not even in high school yet. You're older and wiser, so imagine how much more purposeful and influential your life can be.

I was at a conference a couple of years ago—a gathering of missionaries that work with families. One night a group of teenage girls came on stage and asked for donations toward building a well in Africa. God used that night to open doors for those girls that they never could have imagined. They have since taken multiple mission trips and been part of completing wells in Ghana, India, and Honduras. They've collected and given away over $18,000. And they started this when they were twelve years old.[2]

You may have heard of the twin brothers Alex and Brett Harris and their book *Do Hard Things*. These guys wrote a bestselling book about making the most of your teen years, and they did it when *they* were teens. Their dad pushed them to try new things, take risks, stretch beyond what they thought they could do, and trust God to open doors. They wrote about some of their experiences in the book but also collected stories from other teens.

Alex Harris said this about the teen years:

Responsibility is a muscle. . . . [It] has to be worked out. And if you're not working it out, it's not just static, it's getting weaker.

The Bible says if you're faithful in the little things I'll put you over greater things. That's not a call to a boring life. That's a call to a more and more exciting life. The earlier you start developing that responsibility, the earlier you start being faithful, the sooner those bigger opportunities come along.[3]

That makes sense. In some ways, it's just basic math. The earlier you start investing your life, the more time you have to see God work.

I know someone reading this right now is a gigantic stress ball. You've had pressure on you since preschool to pass potty training 101, and make all A's for the rest of your school life because "Harvard is watching." That would definitely stress me out. And make it harder to go potty. This chapter isn't about that (the stress or the potty). Instead, it's about learning to trust God to use your life for a greater purpose. It's a choice to lift your eyes above the day-to-day toward a bigger vision for life.

Sounds exciting, doesn't it? But wait . . . don't get too excited. Every party needs a pooper, and I guess that person is me. Because before we go full bore on how amazing you're going to be, we've got to talk about some challenges you're probably going to face.

It's a crazy world, because just when you're about to do something epic, like find a cure for cancer or figure out how to turn water into gasoline, the world conspires against you to take you off course. Sometimes it's other people causing the problem, which you can't really control, but there's also plenty of ways you can sabotage yourself and make the "age of opportunity" a real downer.

Here you are, trying to get started on the journey of life, trying to get in your car with your shiny new ID—you're ready to drive—ready to take on the road. You've planned one epic trip, and yet roadblocks, road hazards, and potholes are out there just waiting to ruin it.

So let's see if we can't prepare you to navigate these road hazards so you can stay on that journey and make the most of it. Here are a few that seem typical of the teen years.

Road Hazards

Alcohol and Drugs

I'm sure you've heard all the messages: Don't drink, don't do drugs, it's not good for you. Those public health campaigns have been around for years, but I wonder if they've made a dent in the problem. You and I both know it still happens. So let's try and give reasons WHY you need to be wise. I always like hearing the "why" behind an instruction, that way I can engage my mind and heart and obey beyond "Because I said so."

I was in Rwanda, a small country in east Africa, a few years ago. And I was there teaching at a Bible college. Every morning the director would pull up to the gated guest house in his pickup to pick me up, and we would drive forty-five minutes to the school on the outskirts of town. We had all kinds of time to talk about life, Africa, America, the Bible, church, and the difficult history of Rwanda, a country that experienced a horrific genocide in 1994. We covered it all. He was a charming young man with much to offer.

One day during the drive he asked me, "So what do you think about alcohol?" Now, I had been warned that this was a sensitive topic for the group I was teaching, so I wanted to be extra careful.

I could have trotted out the normal arguments: Some churches teach you it's never okay to touch it. Others say that Jesus drank wine, so just be responsible. But again, I wanted to try and go to the deeper question of "why," so I turned to 1 Corinthians 6:12, where it says, "All things are lawful for me, but not all things are profitable. All things are lawful for me, but I will not be mastered by anything."

This verse is great because it goes to the heart of the issue. Some will focus on the "lawful" and "permissible" part, but whether it's lawful or not isn't stopping everyone from drinking underage. In theory that will guide you till age twenty-one, but then what?

It's the last part of the verse, where he says, "I will not be mastered by anything," that you need to wrap your mind around. And this is where I focused with the guy in Africa, because the issue with alcohol, or anything for that matter, is about *mastery*. Is it mastering you, or exercising control over your life? It goes back to what we talked about in chapter 7: What is your governing authority in life? What will rule over you and direct you?

A number of people who drink alcohol struggle with self-control. Not everyone, of course, but many do. And look, I don't think anyone who starts out drinking alcohol says to themselves, "Boy, I hope to become enslaved to this someday." No, people start out because they genuinely like the way it makes them feel.

Here's a little science lesson. Your brain loves to feel good. And your body uses a chemical in the brain, dopamine, to give your brain those good feelings, like it's been wrapped in Grandma's knit wool blanket and handed a warm mug of hot chocolate with miniature marshmallows floating on a magical layer of foam. Warm fuzzy feelings all over.

So the brain doles out little doses of dopamine all the time—someone smiles at you or gives you a compliment, or you score a basket—you get a small burst of cranial cocoa. Mmm . . .

But here's where alcohol and drugs mess things up. They come in and dump buckets and buckets of hot chocolate all over your noggin. And they cross the line and use jumbo marshmallows. Not even fair. Way more than your body is used to. But boy does it feel good. Until the emergency removal team comes in with their nuclear-powered cocoa extractors. Gone in an instant. Just like that, dopamine drops way below normal levels. That's when addiction steps in. Your brain goes, *Wait a second, I miss my cocoa. And Grandma's blanket. I must find more!* Thus begins an overwhelming impulse to get more.

I've got a friend who is really struggling with alcohol. He would even say he is enslaved. Some mornings he'll start with the hard stuff, and he might stay drunk for a couple of days. He finds his life controlled by the bottle.

I have another friend in his mid-thirties. Maybe that sounds like an eternity away right now, but it's really not all that far off. This friend was very successful in business. He had multiple houses, managed multiple offices, had fancy cars and lots of money. But he lost it all and is dying due to liver failure. This should be the prime of his life, yet it's almost over for him.

He's told me that he remembers the day when drinking went from something he did because he liked the feeling, to something he did because he couldn't function without it.

Now, does that sound like Grandma's hot cocoa? I don't think so.

I'm not saying that will be you if you take a drink. But you need to be very careful about it because it can easily enslave you.

So you don't want to end up mastered by anything. But remember another part of that verse: "Not all things are profitable."

There's a pretty good chance that some of your friends in the next few years will be—and may already be—experimenting with drinking or smoking marijuana or other kinds of drugs. And some of them might encourage you to do so as well. They'll want you to join them, to fit in with the crowd.

Is the "profit" you get from feeling intoxicated and "fitting in" (with the crowd who likes you mainly because you try their drink or drug) worth rejecting God's call on your life to pursue purity and godliness? Will you trust that He knows what's best for you in all situations?

I want to challenge you to make up your mind right now that you're not going to experiment with drugs or alcohol. They're not profitable for you, and you're more likely to be mastered by them if you experiment when you are young.

The thing about drugs that you have to be especially aware of is how CRAZY addictive they are. Many people enjoy a glass of wine here or there and never feel an addictive impulse. But those who experiment with drugs—especially some of the ultra-addictive ones like cocaine and meth—find themselves completely addicted, and sometimes instantaneously. I've got a friend who was addicted to meth, and all it took was one time. She said the moment she took the first hit, it was like her brain flipped on a meth switch and all she could think about was getting that next hit. It felt like her body had found the one thing it had always been looking for, yet it was also the worst thing for her. It was only by God's grace she was able to get off of it.

Part of the reason people take drugs is for the feeling—the sense of peace and calm; it's an escape. It's also risky behavior, and teenage boys especially are drawn to risk. The other day my son was at a friend's house after a paintball game. One of the moms asked the boys, with a hint of trepidation and concern, "Did anyone get hurt?" and the boys responded, "Of course. That's why we go!" And they proceeded to proudly display their pneumatically procured bruises. Risk is like free pizza to a fifteen-year-old boy: He'll find it if it exists. So be extra mindful of this.

Again, I'm not saying that you'd become a meth head with no teeth and sunken cheeks because you popped one pill or pulled one puff from a pipe. But do you really want to go down that path? Every drug you try makes it more likely you'll try something more addictive—to keep the fix going. Do you want to open that door? Is it worth the risk to potentially derail becoming the insanely awesome person God means for you to be?

Okay, so drugs and alcohol—they can definitely be road hazards. There are some other things that can take you off course but might not be quite as obvious, and that's all kinds of time-wasters.

Time-Wasters

Back before electronics, things like *chess* and *reading novels* were the time-wasters (*gasp!*). But now the options seem endless. In this age of the internet and instant information and entertainment, there are *sooo* many things that can hijack your time. You get sucked into an endless string of cat-fail videos or social media posts, or a group text morphs into a new strain of the flu virus, infecting everyone's phone. Or there's the video game that outlasts the annual Christmas monopoly marathon at Uncle Marvin's house. These can all create a mind-numbing wrinkle in time that leaves your brain woozy and the back of your eyeballs itching.

The videos, the social media, and the video games aren't inherently bad, but they sure can eat up huge chunks of time in a hurry.

VIDEO GAMES

Video games are a big temptation when it comes to killing time. Now don't freak out; I'm not saying all video games are evil. But be informed about how much of your life they can consume if you're not wise to how they work.

You've already read how drugs and alcohol affect your brain. Video games kind of do the same thing. It's the steady dose of excitement that amps up the dopamine and creates addiction. Video game designers know this, so they've done their best to make the games unending—you just keep going from level to level to level, higher and higher and higher.

SOCIAL MEDIA AND PHONES

Social media and phones can be like this too. You get sucked into the life of famous people, or the romantic ramblings of a friend, or, like, whatever. You jump back and forth from one "he said" to another "she said" over and over again. Your thumbs even fly like a video game controller. And it's a crazy-maker trying to keep up with which site or app is the best, latest, and greatest, so you check and post to multiple places and people, eating up even more time.

Again, it can be good to use social media to stay connected, but it's a downer when it starts to take over your life and even replace face-to-face.

It seems that phones and social media have taken over our lives. (I'm lumping the two together because they often go hand in hand.) Phones are ridiculously amazing devices that help accomplish all kinds of good. But like an alien invasion, they've taken over our brains and made us unable to think on our own at times.

Do you ever feel like you can't make a decision without your phone in hand? Or do you struggle to finish a ten-minute conversation without checking your phone? What about checking it at church? Oh yeah, you know who you are. I've done it too (don't tell my pastor). And don't try to say you were just reading your Bible.

Why do we do that? Partly because it's easy to find your value in social media, to root your identity in your acceptance. Brian Housman, who wrote a book on this, tells a story of his fourteen-year-old daughter and social media:

> I'm in the living room and then I hear screaming in her bedroom. I get up and run in there [thinking something's wrong] and she's waving her cell phone at me. And she goes: "Look at me! I got my first photo with 100 likes!" Then a few minutes later she said, "I wonder how long it'll take me to get another one?" That feeling of satisfaction was gone in a moment.[4]

Of course, it feels good to be noticed. But it's dangerous to equate approval with significance. Your value is so much greater than the collected approval of others.

Let's pretend you're thinking, *I'm addicted! How do I stop?* I'll toss out a few suggestions, some more radical than others. Don't hyperventilate on me, just pick one or two to try.

- **Turn your phone off at night.** You'll sleep better, and good sleep is the key to a better memory, better grades, fat loss, and muscle growth, all things you're probably interested in.
- **Turn off notifications.** Check info on your terms rather than having it shoved in your face all the time.
- **Wait till after breakfast to check your phone.** That way you'll give your mind time to wake up and connect with God.
- **Take a half-day break once a week.** Use that time to read, talk with your family, exercise, study, or try something new. Sunday afternoons is a perfect time.
- **Be careful what you post.** Once it's posted, it's out there for the world to see. Girls especially need to be aware of this. It's easy to let standards slip over time, show a little more skin, or talk a little more risqué to gain more attention. People do

desperate things when they find their value and worth—and their identity—in the approval of others.

- **Be careful with whom you interact.** A friend of mine mentors a group of girls your age, and she's had several young friends get caught up with a "new" friend only to find out he's twice their age and not looking for a friend, but much more. Creepy. And dangerous.

- **Be accountable.** Have people around you, like your friends and parents, who know your standards and are willing to call you up to them. Your life online should be fully accessible to them. That might sound crazy, but it is a really good thing. Remember that "Successful Independence" thing? They are helping you get there by helping you learn wisdom online. And just knowing they might check will help keep you in check.

- Here's a crazy one: **Leave the phone at home every once in a while.** Hard to imagine, I know, but try it. You might feel naked at first, but before long you'll be unashamed and find it a bit freeing.

- **Create some "phone-free zones."** Like church. Or class. Whenever you need to focus, leave the phone in the car.

- **Keep it facedown during conversations.** When it rings, don't even look at it, just silence it. Let it go to voice mail. That's what it's for. Better yet, keep it in your pocket. Out of sight = out of mind.

Start to regain control over your device and make it serve you instead of you serving it.

Author Kurt Bruner had this to say about video games, but I think it's a great way to think about all social media or online or digital experiences. He says that instead of real life,

> These games provide an artificial replacement—without the risk, without the self-sacrifice. [But instead] we're called to heroic self-sacrifice . . . to whatever the Lord calls us to, and to accomplish

things. And, in video games [and social media], the call to adventure, the call to accomplishment, are all satisfied with no risk. That leads to . . . the lack and loss of joy and satisfaction in life . . . young [people], are missing out on what life was made to be because of this consumption and this compulsion.[5]

These are some of the most amazing years of your life, and you want to enjoy them to the fullest and make the most of them. So you have to choose wisely how to use your time. There are only twenty-four hours in a day, and you can never get back a moment of time.

So watch out for time-wasters—they will rob you of greater opportunities God has for you. Now let's talk about one that is a little more taboo: pornography.

Pornography

This is something that can really get you off track and slowly rob your identity. Guys tend to struggle with porn more than girls, though it is still a challenge for both. I think you probably know it's not good—not for you, not for society, and not for the women and men on screen. We're aware of that truth, but it's still highly addictive. In fact, the addictive power is much like drugs and alcohol. Seems farfetched, but it's true.

Technology allows us to scan the brain to see what parts light up and react to the impulses it experiences. The crazy thing is that a brain on porn scans a lot like a brain on heroin or cocaine. When a person looks at porn, the brain is getting flooded with dopamine just like with drugs. And just like with drugs, when you stop looking at it, the good feelings fade and the cravings kick in.

But there's something else happening in the brain during porn that's different than drugs and alcohol. Just as we mentioned in the dating chapter, your body releases another chemical during sex, a bonding chemical. It's designed to bond you to a person, but with porn you're bonding to a fantasy. God has given us these chemicals in our brains for a good reason—to make a deep emotional bond and connection with a spouse someday. But if you're bonding to a fantasy, you're making it more difficult to bond to a real person. And this has caused some horror stories for newlyweds.

A friend of mine, Brian Goins, who speaks to groups of men about the dangers of porn, shares the story of a young couple that faced this unexpected problem. The guy was twenty-five and had remained a virgin till marriage. But his wedding night did not go as planned. When it came time to have sex with his wife—the woman he had been saving himself for, the moment many dream of—he could not get aroused (have an erection). And that was a big disappointment for both of them. But the story gets even more difficult, because at first he wasn't sure why this happened. So they went to see a doctor. And the doctor, knowing what was probably happening, asks, "Have you been looking at porn?" And now the guy has to come clean to his new wife about his porn addiction right there in the doctor's office.

Your brain is your greatest sexual organ, so if it has been trained to be aroused by porn, it loses the ability to be aroused by anything other than porn. The enemy is the great deceiver; he's the father of lies. And he's good at convincing people that intimacy with an image is good. But it's a false substitute, and it will steal intimacy with a real person from you. Thankfully, this guy and his wife, once he broke away from porn for a while, were able to experience intimacy together.

It's scary to think your wedding night could be wrecked like that. But it's not just your wedding night you need to be concerned about. Most people looking at porn, especially teens, don't feel good about themselves *now*. They know it's not right—it's not honoring to God or the person on the screen. And so it's grating on their conscience, on their soul, and they are conflicted. And that's a tough place to be as well. Who wants that?

Many who are addicted to porn already feel incredibly defeated, like they're trapped and there's no way to win. So how can you win? How can you gain victory?

1. **Tell someone you trust about it.** Sin loves to stay hidden because it grows in the dark, so get it out in the light where others can help you wrestle with it. Could be a pastor, or a friend, or even one of your parents. More than likely they can relate to what you're going through and will help you gain control.

2. **Be willing to do whatever it takes to deal with the device that is bringing you down.** Hand your phone over to a family member after 9 p.m. Never be alone with internet access. Get filters and blockers installed. Check out Covenant Eyes—a ministry that reports your internet use to others. Just as with social media, if you know others are checking, you're more likely to walk carefully and wisely.

3. **Foster a deeper love for Jesus.** There's a great quote from an old Puritan writer, Thomas Chalmers. The key phrase speaks of "the expulsive power of a new affection." You have to find a greater affection, a greater love, that can drive out or "expel" a lesser affection in your life. You've probably experienced this. You might have been totally enamored with a guy or girl at one point, but then completely forgot about them after taking interest in someone else.

If you want to lessen your love of porn, you have to foster an affection that is greater than your love of porn. And that will take time. I think most guys feel like it's impossible to keep from lusting, but this approach will give you a plan of attack that can work, or at least give you some success.

Maybe you've been consuming porn for years and you're filled with shame and guilt. But I want to give you hope. Galatians 5:1 says, "It was for freedom that Christ set us free; therefore keep standing firm and *do not be subject again to a yoke of slavery*" (italics added). There is no better time than now to get free. And you can trust that Christ will set you free from the slavery of lust. That doesn't mean you won't have struggles, but you no longer have to be enslaved.

This is a battle worth fighting—it is worth pursuing purity. Do it for God's glory and for your own protection.

"Fitting In"

Ever feel like you have to compromise your values to fit in with the crowd? I love a quote I've heard Dennis Rainey share: "Life is full of temptations disguised as small choices." Little compromises add up over time, and that changes you. And it's hard to know sometimes if a little decision is really a big decision. But let's deal with the deeper heart issue—are you willing to stand firm in the face of temptation to remain true to your values, even if that means rejection? Or are you more like a chameleon, ready to change your identity in an instant just to fit in with the crowd that gives the acceptance you so desperately crave?

I've seen both girls and boys give in to having sex with someone, even when they didn't want to, because they worried about being rejected. They were worried what people would say if they said no.

If you find yourself feeling like you have to fit in to find significance, stop and ask yourself why. If you're going against your morals to fit in with a crowd, then those probably aren't the people you want to be hanging out with anyway. If they really cared about you, they wouldn't require you to change, they would want to know you for who you are.

There's a shallowness to a person who's desperate for acceptance. You can see that kind of person coming a mile away. And the insecurity repels many of the very people they're trying hard to impress. A healthy level of self-confidence is so much more appealing.

Of course it's natural to want to be accepted, and let's face it, rejection is hard to deal with. But here's an amazing part of the gospel: You are accepted by the God who created the universe. That kind of makes being accepted in gym class seem slightly less significant, doesn't it?

But when we freak out and find our identity in other areas, like acceptance, we can lose sight of our true identity in Christ and who He made us to be.

Cutting/Control Issues

There's one other life-derailer to address before wrapping up this chapter. And it has to do with control. There are a few ways this can play out, and these often end up being more of a problem for young ladies than for young men. We discussed one of these already in the womanhood chapter—eating disorders. But there's another one, and it's hurting more teens than you would think. It's the issue of cutting.

Sharon Hersh, who wrote a book to teen girls, says that "Two million Americans are involved in cutting, self-mutilating behaviors, and almost all started when they were adolescents, and almost all are girls."[6]

She's seen girls who have carved words like *ugly* or *bad* in their arms and legs; some carve intricate designs; others repeat slash after slash in their flesh.

Why would a young girl do this? Especially given how much beauty and body image are worshiped in today's world. Sliced and diced arms and legs aren't part of the standard super-model résumé-building program. And why girls more than boys? Boys seem to enjoy a level of pain in the context of games or competitive sports.[7] Yet many young women your age are turning to cutting to alleviate pain, especially from loss or rejection. Girls in particular appear to be more vulnerable to the affects of loss. Sharon listed some specific losses to watch out for:

- Loss of a close friend—a confidant with whom you can share true feelings.
- Loss of being a little girl. Many girls resist growing up and developing a female body and the responsibilities that come with that—eating disorders are often a response to that.

- The loss of belonging.
- The loss of a family, or a broken family.
- The loss of middle school life.

These losses are certainly difficult to navigate, but why does cutting your skin help alleviate the pain? Seems like that would add *more* pain. Sharon said that psychologically, cutting creates a connection between the emotional pain and the physical pain . . . followed by a sense of relief and numbness immediately after the cut. And just like with other numbing activities like drugs and alcohol, that feeling can be addictive.

There's another aspect I didn't quite understand until a friend explained it to me. Michelle Hill, who has mentored girls your age for years, has thought a lot about this. She says the fact that cutting is connected to control was a huge insight for her. She explained,

> Often when we do things that we otherwise would never think of doing—like cutting ourselves, or starving ourselves, or even something like manipulating a boy—we're tempted to do these things because *we want control*. It's kind of a desperation move, where we feel like life is out of control so we just need to control something, anything. This is why it's so important to remember your identity as a child of God. Whenever things feel out of control, and you feel desperate, remember that God is in control. Always.[8]

Whenever I've felt out of control in life, it's almost always because of trying to control too much. But when I hand over my anxieties, my fears, my compulsions, to God, to someone a million times more capable to handle them than me, then the overwhelming need to be in control of everything melts away, and in their place rush joy and peace.

Memorizing Scripture has also been one of the most important ways to overcome fear, anxiety, and control. Here's a verse that has meant so much to me.

Come to Me [Jesus], all who are weary and heavy-laden, and I will give you rest. Take My yoke upon you and learn from Me, for I am gentle and humble in heart; and you will find rest for your souls. For My yoke is easy and My burden is light.

Matthew 11:28–30

Everyone wants rest. Everyone wants the pain and hurt to depart. Things like cutting or eating disorders may bring a temporary rest or relief, but the ultimate rest will only be found in Christ—by rooting your identity in Him.

Stay on the Road

These are all challenges and temptations that can derail your pursuit of your true identity. Of course, there are other things out there, but these are some of the main hazards teens encounter. What I'd encourage you to do, if you are struggling in any of these areas, is to start finding help now. Don't wait. Now is the time. More than likely these struggles won't completely go away on their own, so take them seriously and enlist people and the power of the Holy Spirit to guide you through this season.

14

Finding Your Mission in Life

So we've said these years can be a really amazing time for you, and we've warned of the tire shredders that can put a downer on the road trip of life. Now, how do we figure out your mission or purpose? What are you supposed to do with the rest of your life? Is it artist or accountant? Pro basketball player or fly-fishing guide? Construction worker or engineer? English teacher or writer? How do you figure this out, and how does one keep from "screwing up" life by making a wrong decision? (Hint: You probably won't.)

This can all feel a bit overwhelming. But you don't have to figure it all out today. It's a process. Maybe back in the 1950s someone would do the same job for forty years, but the world doesn't really work that way anymore. Even if you work for the same company your entire adult life, you'll likely hold dozens of different jobs, some of which might look nothing like what you started out doing.

So let's begin with some foundational principles about work and life and how they relate.

Life Is Not Primarily About You

It's true. Life is not first and foremost about you. You and I, we're just a small piece of humanity that is alive today. And we're an even smaller slice—in fact, almost negligible—of the entirety of human existence. Don't let this make you feel like your life doesn't matter. Instead, I'm hoping that it helps lift your eyes off yourself and sets you thinking about what God wants for this world and how you can be a part of that.

You Are Made for Good Works

Ephesians 2:10 says, "We are His workmanship, created in Christ Jesus for good works, which God prepared beforehand so that we would walk in them." We can know, with confidence, that God already has great things in store for us. He's not sitting behind a giant curtain, wringing His hands, wondering if there's anything for you in this world. No, He already has things in mind for you to do. It might be hard to figure it out and it might take some time—just like He put diamonds underground that take work to unearth—but you can know in advance that the struggle will be worth it.

Delight to Light the Path

Psalm 37:4 says, "Delight yourself in the Lord; and He will give you the desires of your heart." To figure out God's desires for you, start by delighting in Him. And as you delight in Him, He will open your eyes to the desires of your heart. He will align your heart with the gifts and talents He has given you to serve the world. But the first step is to delight *in Him*. Trouble starts when we turn this upside down, i.e., delighting in other things and then trying to tack God on afterwards. God can certainly still use that person, but it can be messy.

Business Glorifies God

Wayne Grudem wrote a book called *Business to the Glory of God.* He was attempting to show how business, assuming that it's not engaged in sinful practices or industries, is inherently good because it adds value to mankind. If I start a business making the best shoes ever, and I sell them to you, and you buy them from me, then we both benefit. You received something that made your feet happy, and I received money to live on in return and to fund my business to create more killer apparel. This makes the world a better place, which glorifies God.

Vocation vs. Mission

I was walking in the woods once with a young man who had questions about life. He was wondering what kind of work he should do. As a Christian, he was struggling with whether he should go into business or full-time ministry. He's a gifted musician and was leading worship at his church. But he also loved programming and was considering a job in that field. He wondered if a job in business would be less meaningful to God than serving in ministry. So here's what I explained.

There's a difference between *vocation* and *mission*. Every Christian is called to be "on mission" for God. And that mission is often called "the great co-mission," found in Matthew 28:19–20, which says, "Go therefore and make disciples of all nations, baptizing them in the name of the Father and the Son and the Holy Spirit, teaching them to observe all that I commanded you; and lo, I am with you always, even to the end of the age." All Christians are to be involved in "making disciples of all nations." That's the major mission of your life—to make Christ known to the world. And there's lots of ways you can go about that.

Although that's the same mission we all share, we don't all have the same vocation. I define *vocation* pretty simply: How do you make money for living? There's other ways to define it, and your vocation shouldn't sum up everything about you, but that's how I'll define it here. And there's a whole host of vocations out there, or "jobs." You could do anything from scooping manure out of the lion's cage at the zoo (good luck getting insurance for that) to being CEO of IBM. A wide, wide range of jobs. And when you look in the Bible, you don't really see one job being listed as way more important than others. In fact, in ancient Israel, you couldn't be a priest unless you had the last name Levi. But the Levites didn't seem to be seen as more special than the other tribes. In fact, God was pretty hard on them at times.

No, serving in ministry doesn't make you a better person or more special to God. And it doesn't inherently make God happier. In fact, I've known people who serve in ministry for the wrong reasons: They want the feeling of power over other people, they love being in front of a crowd, or they might even want to show off their Bible knowledge to feel important. These motivations are the opposite of what ministry should be about.

It seems that Paul saw his vocation as merely a vehicle for reaching people who needed to know Jesus. Sometimes he made tents, sometimes he was a travel channel correspondent, and other times he was a professional prisoner. But it was all about the MISSION. The mission informed his vocation.

So now that we've covered some guiding principles, let's talk about how to figure out your vocation.

I think it is really pretty simple. Simple doesn't mean easy, though—but it boils down to just a few things:

1. What do you love?
2. What are you good at?
3. What gives people value?

If you can figure out those three things, you'll end up figuring out how to make money at it. Don't worry if there's not a job market for your skill set yet. If you figure out those three things, I guarantee you'll make enough money to live on and even flourish.

That's simple, but it might take a long time to figure it out. A great starting point is the message of a book summed up in the title *Just Do Something*. Get started. At what? I don't know. You tell me. Think about those questions. What are you good at? Or what do you love? Find that thing and figure out how to do it in a way that gives value to others. Too many folks are waiting for the perfect situation. They don't want just any job—they want the perfect job. But there is no perfect job. And every job done well, no matter how small, opens the door for the next thing. Every job or project is an interview or résumé. I love the quote by Dennis Rainey I mentioned before, "The best measure of what a man can do is what he has done." If you do the little things well, people notice, and it opens new doors.

Josh Harris became a really popular Christian author and speaker when he wrote the book *I Kissed Dating Goodbye*. He was just a couple of years older than you at the time. It seemed that every Christian looking to date was reading that book and talking about it. Some loved it, some scoffed at it, but everyone knew about it. But Josh didn't all of a sudden start writing one day and the book just appeared on shelves. It started when he was a boy, being homeschooled by his mom. His parents noticed that he had an interest in writing. So his dad encouraged him to start a newsletter to other homeschool students. And that took off. That led to opportunities to write articles for magazines. Eventually he tried other creative endeavors like video production. And he learned something from each of these ventures, so that when it came time to write a book, he had the experience to finish a big project like that, even though he was only eighteen.

There really is no lost effort, even if nothing seems to come of it. You just have to keep walking through the doors as they open, but it starts with doing something.

Lovers and Haters

As you get started doing something, you'll get two kinds of feed-back. One will be real specific—"tweak that color" or "use stronger verbs" or "put more spin on your shot." Those are really helpful, especially if the person giving the feedback knows what they're talking about. Take that feedback with extreme gratitude. Figure out how to tweak what you're doing. That's gold.

Focus on building the skills you're developing. No skills are wasted, and no one can take your skills away from you. Like we talked about earlier in the book, to get skills, you have to practice like mad. How much? There's something called the 10,000 hour rule that gets tossed around a bit.[1] Some say it takes that long, that much effort and practice, to become an expert in a field. Is it exactly 10,000 hours? I don't know. But your guitar won't play itself. Your picture won't paint itself. The app won't create itself. Do more and you'll learn more about what you're good at, what you like, and what gives value to people. Those efforts will pay off at some point, even if you can't imagine how. Proverbs 22:29 says, "Do you see a man skilled in his work? He will stand before kings; he will not stand before obscure men." Build skills and doors will open. People will take notice. And before long, you'll have a better sense of what it is you want to do with your life.

While you're young, while you have tons of time on your hands, get busy creating. Draw a picture every day. Even if the first one stinks. I guarantee your one-hundredth picture will be better than your first. Or write a blog post every day. Or take five hundred shots, or two hundred swings, or one hundred photos. Whatever it is, put in the work. It will pay off and the effort will guide you.

I loved to draw in high school. But my drawings were just okay. Don't worry, I'm man enough to admit it. I really liked art but needed to work hard to get better. But for some reason I didn't see it that way. Instead I thought, *I'm really average at drawing. I don't have the talent like some of these other guys. I'm just going to do what's needed to get by in class. No one would ever pay me money to draw. I'll never be good enough to be a professional artist.* Wow. Captain Positive. I've since done some drawings that were okay—not amazing—but it's obvious now that if I would have worked hard at it, the right doors would have opened. And as you grow your skills, you'll also start to notice those opportunities.

Talent is of some value; it helps get you started. But hard work wins out over talent eventually. If you have middle-of-the-road talent, you'll eventually surpass a talented-but-doesn't-work-on-it person. I've seen it time and again.

There's another kind of feedback you'll get. It's the haters. They'll say you're terrible, that you're not good enough. *Ignore* those people. They are mostly jealous and don't want you succeeding. Just keep doing what you're doing. Keep creating. There will come a day when others will notice that you are improving. There really will. But keep working, and block out the haters. Listen to wisdom—even if it's hard to hear—that is shared in love. It will make you better.

So let's take a stab at figuring out your vocation. Go ahead and write some things down here to help get you started. Write down three things in each of the categories.

I love to:

_____

People say I'm good at:

_____

I give value to people by:

_____

Vocation as Mission

Now, once you get a better idea of your vocation, you should ask God how He can use your vocation to accomplish His mission. It might be obvious or you might need a ton of guidance.

I have a friend who loves coffee. Man, is he nuts about coffee. Or, I should say, beans about coffee . . . (sigh). He started learning all about coffee—how to roast, grind, brew—all the best ways. But he also wanted to be a missionary in top-secret countries. Like a Christian spy. Well, what do you know, one day he realized he could go to these countries that wouldn't let Christian missionaries in by opening coffee houses. And the best part of a coffee house (well, besides good coffee) is that people come to you, and it's a great place to strike up a conversation. He now has a captive audience in a foreign country in a way he never could have imagined. But it came out of fostering his desires.

Your mission and vocation are an important part of your life, and God will use them both to make the world a better place. And it may take a while to really figure out how He has designed you. That's okay. Just keep working hard at building skills with things you love, and He'll use that to open the next door.

The Journey Continues

Think back to the beginning of this book, where I asked you to write down a few words that summed up who you are, that you would use to describe yourself to someone else. Look back real quick at those in chapter 1. What do you still think about those? After reading through an entire book on identity, how do you think about them now? Do they still sum up your identity? Do they still seem as important as they did?

When I was a sophomore in high school, I had my list of things that defined me: church youth group, jean jacket, a little bit of school (mostly chemistry), my Ocean Pacific T-shirts (both of them), my car, Christian heavy metal music, backpacking, and working hard at the grocery store. (Stop laughing, please.)

Five years later it was about finishing engineering school, doing ministry with college students, lifting weights, and thinking about asking my girlfriend to marry me. No OP T-shirts (thank goodness) and no jean jacket.

Five years after that it was being a good husband, having good office attire, developing best business practices, learning to be a better writer, fly-fishing, and reading. Lots of reading. No engineering. No college students.

Here's the point.

Some of the main things that defined my identity changed year after year. Sometimes in big ways. And sometimes within just a few years my life looked completely different.

Think back to just a couple of years ago. How different were your interests? Which of the things you identified at the beginning were on your radar back then? Some were, but I bet some weren't.

Every year your identity morphs, develops, and grows. And if your identity is rooted too much in any one of these things, you might hit a big identity crisis when things change.

And though my life has experienced lots of change, there was one commonality across all the stages mentioned above. And it wasn't Christian heavy metal. It was that my *true* identity was rooted in Christ.

My prayer for you is that this book would help you do the same. The teen years are full of some crazy times. Crazy amounts of change. Hormones, pressures, challenges, likes, dislikes, so much. But lots of excitement as well—lots of fun. And an amazing season of discovery.

Whatever you discover about your mission and your relationships, whatever friends you find, whatever your family is like, and how you live out being a young man or woman, you have to root your life in the main thing: your relationship to Christ. He will never let you down. He will never fail you. Through Him your identity will be secured regardless of how your life changes. Through Him you will discover your true identity and have the confidence to live it out now and in all the years ahead.

Acknowledgments

Thanks to Dennis Rainey for pushing me to write many years ago. To Bob Lepine for helping me grow as a content creator. To Wayne Grudem for teaching me to think critically and to write clearly. To Bruce Goff, Dan Sheaffer, and Michelle Hill for shaping the content of Passport2Identity, the basis for this book. Tim Grissom for the camaraderie I didn't know writers could share. Leslie Barner for all your insight on design and your amazing leadership of the publishing team at FamilyLife. To Joe Teeter: the Little House made the difference.

For the teens who took the time to read the manuscript and provide feedback: Lily, Liz, Carson, and Anastasia—your insights and encouragement were a huge addition.

For the families who have faithfully supported us in ministry for so many years. For my parents who shaped so much of my identity and have been my biggest cheerleaders. Thanks for not letting me get away with sloppy writing and for not giving up on me. And to Julie, my bride, I wouldn't even think of touching a keyboard without your loving correction in my life. You taught me to be teachable in so many ways. I love you and love living life with you. I pray the teens who read this book are fortunate enough to find a spouse with the character, Christ-centered mind-set, and sacrificial love that you live out every day.

Additional Resources

Mark Hamby, founder of Lamplighter Ministries, said a turning point in his Christian growth occurred when he was challenged by an older man to read more Christian biographies. He said, "Biographies were the catalysts God used in my life to inspire and instill a love for reading. I still quote from these literary treasures, and I still pray the prayers of these giants of the faith. I consider them my mentors and seek to follow their example."

Hamby recommends the following biographies to get started: Amy Carmichael; George Muller; Gladys Aylward; D. L. Moody; Hudson Taylor; *Behind Mr. Bunyan* by Agnes Beaumont; *If I Perish* by I-suk An; and *Bruchko* by Bruce Olson. All eight are available through Lamplighter Publishing.

R. Kent Hughes, author of *Disciplines of a Godly Man*, conducted a survey of a number of Christian leaders, asking what were the most influential books they had read. After the Bible, the following were some of the most often mentioned.

Mere Christianity by C. S. Lewis. Written by the author of THE CHRONICLES OF NARNIA, this book appeals to reason and paints a clear and concise picture of the essence of

Christianity. Other than the Bible, there's been no book that's had as much influence on shaping my life as this one.

In His Steps by Charles Sheldon. Written in the late 1800s, it is the story of a man who takes seriously the question, "What Would Jesus Do?"

Institutes of the Christian Religion by John Calvin. Calvin submitted a copy of his writings to the king of France in an effort to persuade him to adopt the "new" beliefs of the Reformation. Though a long book, it's surprisingly readable and edifying.

My Utmost for His Highest by Oswald Chambers. Many in my church kept this daily devotional next to their Bible. I found it over my head at first. But when I returned to it later, my heart was ready to absorb the depths it offered. Its beauty is in its brevity, at one small page and one verse per day.

War and Peace and *Anna Karenina* by Leo Tolstoy. Two epic works of literature by a Russian writer. Both have had a huge amount of influence. And both are huge, coming in at over eight hundred pages.

Shadow of the Almighty by Elisabeth Elliot. Incredible story of how God worked through Jim and Elisabeth Elliot and other young missionaries to reach a remote people group in Ecuador. Their martyrdom by those very people they tried to reach was a great tragedy yet also launched a powerful missions movement. It definitely stirred me to consider what God had in store for my future.

Hudson Taylor's Spiritual Secret by Dr. and Mrs. Howard Taylor. A biography of the famous missionary who worked in China in the 1800s. What stood out was how Taylor, as a young man in America, focused his life around preparing for the hardships of the mission field in remote China. He created difficult living conditions for himself (like sleeping on the floor) and began learning Chinese by comparing an English Bible to a Chinese Bible. It's rare to run across someone who has such focus and clarity of purpose at such a young age.

The Imitation of Christ by Thomas à Kempis, a German monk from the 1400s. It's amazing how often this work is mentioned by other spiritual giants, like C. S. Lewis. No coincidence, since it is thought to be the most widely read and translated Christian devotional work of all time.

The Great Divorce by C. S. Lewis. This book blew my mind. Especially his depiction of those who are in hell and why they are there. The imagery of the lizard locked onto the shoulder of one of the characters reminded me of Eustace (from Narnia) and his own lizard skin predicament. I left the book praying that I would be able to get my eyes off myself and avoid endless empty prattle and self-delusionment modeled by many on the bus.

Confessions by St. Augustine. An autobiography of the early church's most influential theologian. This focuses on his personal journey from rejecting Christ to embracing faith. I couldn't believe that such an iconic figure of church history could be so candid about his own struggles. So many will relate to his battle with sin.

Notes

Section One: Who Am I?

1. Alexandra Leigh Young, "The Girl Who Doesn't Exist," Radiolab podcast, August 29, 2016, http://www.radiolab.org/story/invisible-girl/.

Chapter 1: What Is Identity?

1. "Tim Keller | Our Identity: The Christian Alternative to Late Modernity's Story," YouTube video, 36:45, November 11, 2015, Posted by Wheaton College, https://www.youtube.com/watch?v=Ehw87PqTwKw. Dr. Keller also discussed this topic in his book *Making Sense of God* (New York: Viking, 2016), 126–127.

2. I will try to use the word *sex* when referring to biology and *gender* when referring to the cultural expectations for the sexes.

3. Eighty-five percent more. Statistics from Michael J. Rosen, *Girls vs. Guys: Surprising Differences Between the Sexes* (Minneapolis: Twenty-First Century Books, 2014), 8–9.

4. Ibid., 22–23.

5. Leonard Sax, *Why Gender Matters* (New York: Doubleday, 2005), 18–22.

6. Paul Kengor, "The Intellectual Origins of Ronald Reagan's Faith," The Heritage Foundation, April 30, 2004, http://www.heritage.org/political-process/report/the-intellectual-origins-of-ronald-reagans-faith. This article mistakenly refers to the main character as Dick Walker.

Chapter 2: The Ultimate Source of Identity

1. Rick Warren, "Embrace Your Identity in Christ," Pastor Rick's Daily Hope, May 21, 2014, http://pastorrick.com/devotional/english/embrace-your-identity-in-christ.

Chapter 3: Independence without Isolation

1. Crawford Loritts Jr., *Never Walk Away* (Chicago: Moody Publishers, 1997), 72. This quote is a variation of what Benjamin Franklin wrote in *Poor Richard's Almanack*: "Experience keeps a dear school, but fools will learn in no other."

2. David Kaczynski, *Every Last Tie: The Story of the Unabomber and His Family* (Durham, NC: Duke University Press, 2016).

3. Andrew Sharp, "Kobe Bryant Is Not Totally Human, and Now We Have (More) Proof," *SB Nation*, March 6, 2013, http://www.sbnation.com/nba/2013 /3/6/4071142/kobe-bryant-las-vegas-workout-reddit.

Section Two: Gender Identity: What Does It Mean to Be a Man or a Woman?

Chapter 4: The Essence of Manhood

1. Preston Gillham, *Things Only Men Know* (Eugene, OR: Harvest House, 1999), 82.

2. David McCullough, *Truman* (New York: Simon & Schuster, 1992), 123.

3. Alan Scholes, *Enjoying God* (Peachtree City, GA: Campus Crusade for Christ, 2010), see chapter 2 of the book.

4. Martin Blumenson, *Patton* (New York: William Morrow, 1985), 55.

Chapter 5: The Essence of Womanhood

1. Russell Moore, *Passport2Identity for Young Women*, audio CD (FamilyLife, 2016).

2. Ibid.

3. Ibid.

4. M. G. Zimeta, "In John Lewis," *London Review of Books* blog, September 13, 2016, https://www.lrb.co.uk/blog/2016/09/13/mg-zimeta/in-john-lewis/.

5. Russell Moore, *Passport2Identity for Young Women*.

6. Ibid.

7. Ibid.

8. Ibid.

9. John Piper, "Following the Call of Christ," *FamilyLife Today*, July 4, 2011, http://familylifetoday.com/program/following-the-call-of-christ-3/.

10. Ibid.

11. Russell Moore, *Passport2Identity for Young Women*.

Chapter 6: Between Two Worlds: The Transgender Question

1. Allan Metcalf, quoted in *We Cannot Be Silent* by R. Albert Mohler Jr. (Nashville: Thomas Nelson, 2015), 78.

Section Three: Spiritual Identity: The Main Thing

1. David Kinnaman, *You Lost Me* (Grand Rapids, MI: Baker Publishing Group, 2011), 22.

Chapter 7: Making Your Faith Your Own

1. The term *moralistic therapeutic deism* was introduced by Christian Smith in his book *Soul Searching: The Religious and Spiritual Lives of American Teenagers* (New York: Oxford University Press, 2009), 163.

2. Francis Schaeffer, *How Should We Then Live?* (Wheaton, IL: Crossway, 2005), 23.

3. To read more of Nabeel Qureshi's story, see his book *Seeking Allah, Finding Jesus* (Grand Rapids, MI: Zondervan, 2014).

Chapter 8: Growing in Your Walk with God

1. Here are a few good ones on spiritual disciplines: *The Spiritual Disciplines of the Christian Life* by Donald S. Whitney; *The Life You've Always Wanted* by John Ortberg; *Disciplines of a Godly Man* by R. Kent Hughes; *Disciplines of a Godly Woman* by Barbara Hughes; and *Practical Religion* by J. C. Ryle (though written over a hundred years ago, it reads like it was written this decade).

2. Don Whitney, "Governed by God's Word," *FamilyLife Today*, January 6, 2004, http://familylifetoday.com/program/governed-by-god-s-word/.

3. "The Essential 100 Bible Reading Plan," http://scriptureunionresources .com/e100.

4. "The Discipleship Journal Bible Reading Plan," (NavPress, 2005), http:// www.navigators.org/www_navigators_org/media/navigators/tools/Resources /Discipleship-Journal-Bible-Reading-Plan-9781617479083.pdf.

5. We also read through Dietrich Bonhoeffer's book *The Cost of Discipleship*, which is a book about the Sermon on the Mount. It's broken up into sections so that you can read part of the Sermon on the Mount and then read the corresponding chapter in his book to gain greater understanding.

6. Whitney, "Governed by God's Word."

7. Read more about this in Don Whitney's book *Praying the Bible* (Wheaton, IL: Crossway, 2015).

8. Evan Andrews, "7 Early Robots and Automatons," History.com, October 28, 2014, http://www.history.com/news/history-lists/7-early-robots-and-automatons.

9. Read his wife, Edith's, account of their ministry in the book titled, *L'Abri*.

10. Harold Lindsell, *The Battle for the Bible* (Grand Rapids, MI: Zondervan, 1976), 142.

Section Four: Relational Identity: The People Who Shape You

1. Various sources cite Jim Rohn for this quote, including Kai Sato, "Why the Five People Around You Are Crucial to Your Success," *Entrepreneur*, May 9, 2014, https://www.entrepreneur.com/article/233444.

Chapter 9: Friends

1. Sebastian Junger, *WAR* (New York: Hachette, 2010), 239.
2. Leonard Sax, *Girls on the Edge* (New York: Basic Books, 2010), 6.

Chapter 10: Mentors

1. See the list of resources I included in the back of this book.
2. I've also included this list in the Additional Resources section. Look it over and circle one that you can get started reading right away.

Chapter 11: Romance and Dating

1. Gerald Hiestand and Jay Thomas, *Sex, Dating, and Relationships* (Wheaton, IL: Crossway, 2012), 58–59.
2. Russell Moore, *Passport2Identity for Young Women.*
3. Tongue firmly planted in cheek . . .
4. Adapted from a devotional from *Passport2Identity Travel Journal* (Little Rock, AR: FamilyLife, 2013), 102–103.

Chapter 12: Same-Sex Attraction

1. Russell Moore, *Passport2Identity for Young Women.*
2. Ibid.
3. I recommend her book *Secret Thoughts of an Unlikely Convert.* Also Sam Allberry's book, *Is God Anti-Gay?*
4. All quotes in here come from my personal interview with Rosaria, some of which appears on Russell Moore, *Passport2Identity for Young Women,* audio CD.

Section Five: Missional Identity: A Bright Future

Chapter 13: The Age of Opportunity and Road Hazards

1. Russell Moore, *Passport2Identity for Young Women.*
2. A Single Drop Ministry, https://asingledropministry.com/about/.
3. *Stepping Up* Video Series (Little Rock, AR: FamilyLife Publishing, 2012).
4. Russell Moore, *Passport2Identity for Young Women.*
5. Quoted in "Playstation Nation," FamilyLife Today, http://familylifetoday.com/series/playstation-nation/.
6. Sharon Hersh, "Understanding Teen Depression," *FamilyLife Today,* March 2, 2005, http://familylifetoday.com/program/understanding-teen-depression/.
7. See examples in chapter 4 of Leonard Sax, *Why Gender Matters* (New York: DoubleDay, 2005).
8. Quoted in Russell Moore, *Passport2Identity,* audio CD.

Chapter 14: Finding Your Mission in Life

1. See Malcolm Gladwell, *Outliers* (New York: Little Brown, 2013).

John C. Majors creates resources for FamilyLife (a ministry of Cru), like *Passport2Identity*, and has contributed to THE ART OF MARRIAGE video series, the STEPPING UP video series, and Passport2Purity.

John teaches for Cru across the United States and in other countries, training Cru staff in communication and Bible study. He also speaks at FamilyLife's Weekend to Remember events, as well as churches and men's groups on a consistent basis. John and his family live in Little Rock, Arkansas.